Benjamin Franklin

*A Captivating Guide to an American
Polymath and a Founding Father of the
United States of America*

Free Bonus from Captivating History (Available for a Limited time)

Hi History Lovers!

Now you have a chance to join our exclusive history list so you can get your first history ebook for free as well as discounts and a potential to get more history books for free! Simply visit the link below to join.

Captivatinghistory.com/ebook

Also, make sure to follow us on Facebook, Twitter and Youtube by searching for Captivating History.

Contents

Introduction

Benjamin Franklin was a Founding Father of America and had an enormous impact on America as it is today. In addition to that, there are many little-known facts about the man who was Benjamin Franklin. Unlike many of the other Founding Fathers, he started out in humble circumstances. Franklin never finished college because his parents couldn't afford it. He hated his first job, and when he did get another one, he left without notice. He also took off from home without a word to his parents. Yes, Ben Franklin had money, but that ran out, and he wandered the streets of New Jersey and Pennsylvania broke and homeless. He, who once had pipe dreams of becoming a sailor, was shipwrecked near the coast of New York. Franklin was incredibly naïve as a young man. He could be easily fooled and was—on more than one occasion.

As an adult, he captivated the intellectuals of the day. His best friends were doctors, noted chemists, professors, philosophers, scientists, inventors, politicians, and authors. Benjamin Franklin's name is recorded in the National Archives of Great Britain and France as well as in the Library of Congress in the United States. He was a polymath with remarkable skills. Franklin was a writer, a scientist, a postmaster, a printer, a diplomat, and an inventor. One of his well-known inventions was the lightning rod, but the governor of

Pennsylvania refused to install it. His mansion was in fact later struck by lightning!

There are plenty of rumors about him in the history books, and some are true. In 1998, skeletons were found buried in his basement! No, he wasn't a deranged murderer, but there was a sane and logical explanation for it. There were always logical reasons for his every action, but Benjamin Franklin was a unique person who was lost in the beginning but found himself and fulfilled his destiny.

From a young age, Benjamin Franklin fought for the rights of America at home and abroad. Yet, he bore the burdens of leadership and never shirked nor faltered in his mission. His greatest asset was his charm and friendliness, but he had his detractors as well, and felt the emotional impact of that.

Benjamin Franklin had enormous psychological and intellectual energy and worked every day until a week before he died at the age of 84. His impact on the future of America was unparalleled.

Chapter 1 – Young, Earnest, and Foolhardy

The Early Years 1713-1723

As a young boy, Benjamin reported every day to an odoriferous little shop run by his father, Josiah Franklin, at the corner of Hanover and Union Streets in colonial Boston. There, he made soap and candles. Carefully, he poured the hot fat of slaughtered sheep into narrow wooden molds and placed a frame on top with wicks he had made. Even in winter, the shop was hot and smoky. As he worked at the family trade, Ben's gaze strayed outside and he dreamed of traveling in those grand clipper ships across the ocean like his older half-brother, Josiah Jr., a sailor for the British Navy.

If he ran off to sea like Josiah Jr., Benjamin could climb up to a position on the topgallant yardarm and check out the horizon for miles and miles around. Instead of smelling putrid animal fat melting in his father's shop, he could smell the cool salt air and test the wind direction—oh, if only he was a sailor!

When he was 11 years old, Franklin had become an avid swimmer and wanted to design something that would help him move along faster in the water. He then created a pair of swim fins. They weren't used on one's feet, however; they were designed to be attached to the hands. This was his first real invention. In his autobiography of 1773, he wrote: "When a youth, I made two oval pallets, each about ten inches long, and six broad, with a hole for the thumb, in order to retain it fast in the palm of my hand."

A sailor's life would release him from a family where he had to live with fourteen other siblings still at home. Fortunately, the members of the Franklin household related well to each other. Of his early childhood upbringing, Benjamin once wrote:

> It was indeed a lowly dwelling that we were brought up in, but we were fed plentifully, made comfortable with fire and clothing, had seldom any contention among us, but all was harmonious, especially between the heads (parents), and they were universally respected—and the most of the family in good reputation—this is still happier than multitudes enjoy.

The house was small, so it was an overcrowded and noisy home. Benjamin was nearing the age that he could enroll in the British Navy, but his parents wanted a better life for him. Most young boys at sea were abused by the other sailors, and many of them were orphans or delinquents. Benjamin was smart and thought independently. Both his mother, Abiah, and his father knew he was unhappy in the candle and soap-making business.

His parents thought that Benjamin would make a fine minister. Toward that end, they had him enrolled in the Boston Latin School, but he didn't finish because they didn't have the money to keep paying his tuition, and Benjamin didn't show any interest in life as a clergyman anyway. In lieu of that, Josiah realized that Benjamin must have a trade to pursue. So, he took him to his Uncle Samuel's shop. Samuel was a cutler who made knives and other fine-edged tools. Franklin showed some interest in this, but Sam wanted Josiah to pay a fee for his apprenticeship. Ben could have become indentured instead, but that would bind him under contract, and Josiah felt that there might be better opportunities for him. Besides,

Ben hadn't demonstrated any extraordinary ability in working with his hands.

Benjamin's half-brother, Josiah Jr., was lost at sea in the year 1715, so perhaps that wiped out any future consideration of such a dangerous career. Ben never brought up joining the navy again. Fortuitously, his other older brother, James, had recently returned from England where he had learned the printing business. Upon his return, James got a printing press and typesetting trays, and set up a print shop. He published a newspaper there called the *New England Courant*. Benjamin was a voracious reader by nature, having read every book in his father's small library, though many of them, in Ben's words, "were dry-as-dust religious texts except for Rev. Cotton Mather's *Essays to Do Good*." While a boy, he read *Plutarch's Lives* and John Bunyan's collection, which he purchased after reading *Pilgrim's Progress*. Ben was a lover of history as well and also bought Clarence Burton's *Historical Collection*.

When Ben saw the print shop and its newspaper, he was very interested, and his father was pleased. Because Josiah couldn't afford to pay for an apprenticeship, he indentured Benjamin to James. Benjamin would have to work for a number of years at the print shop, but it afforded him the chance to learn the trade from his brother.

This also meant Ben would get a stipend. He temporarily became a vegetarian at that time and discovered that the elimination of meat from his diet left him enough money to rent a room over the shop. There, he set up a library of his own, which grew very large in time.

Alias Silence Dogood

Twenty-two-year-old James was like most young lads at that age, headstrong and opinionated. To James, Benjamin was a mere child, dependent and devoid of ideas. That wasn't true, however. Even as a young adolescent, Benjamin had ambitions of his own, and he was passionate about writing. So, Benjamin went to work for James but had to start out at the entry level and work as a "printer's devil." In time, Ben hoped to have his own byline.

Benjamin was a great help to his brother, but, according to historians, James was very demanding and unreasonable. Consequently, they had a lot of arguments. On a number of occasions, Benjamin's father even had to referee their disputes when they became overheated. Usually, Josiah took Benjamin's side in the frequent arguments.

While he worked at the print shop, Ben borrowed books from his other friends in the printing business, but had to return them rapidly because the books were intended for delivery to a third party. There was no such thing as a lending library in those days. Benjamin was always punctual in returning books and that added incentive made him a speed reader.

Benjamin really wanted to try his hand at writing some letters to be included in James' *New England Courant*. When he asked his brother if he could, James adamantly refused. Still determined to get his work in print and read the readers' reactions, he started mailing a series of letters to the paper in 1722 under the pseudonym "Silence Dogood," a fabricated widow. Ben was extremely prolific and sent in other letters under the amusing pseudonyms, "Anthony Afterwit" and "The Busy Body." People loved them, and the circulation of the *New England Courant* soared. When Ben proudly announced his authorship, James was furious and seething with jealousy. James himself then anonymously wrote editorials that occasionally criticized the English authorities in the colonies. In one reflection about problems with the Indian population in Canada, the paper criticized the way in which the English authorities there were handling the matter. In the *Courant*, it said:

> If Almighty God will have Canada subdued without the assistance of those miserable savages, in whom we have too much confidence, we shall be glad that there will be no

sacrifices offered up to the devil upon the occasion, God alone will have the glory.

Editorials were James' forte, and the *New England Courant* became one of the most read papers in Boston. Then, the governor of Massachusetts Bay Colony, Samuel Shute, found out about the editorials. He vehemently objected to some of those opinion pieces and the matter was referred to the Massachusetts General Court. As a result, poor James and even Benjamin were arrested. Because the Court indicated that the editorials cited some references in the Bible, they labeled them a perversion of the Holy Scriptures. It was suspected that the real reason for the governor's vindictiveness stemmed from the governor's disagreements with the colony and other British officials. Governor Shute was known to have many arguments with the Massachusetts Assembly and frequently suspended their sessions without just cause. He was also negligent in providing for the defense of the colony, which was a requirement he was supposed to fulfill, and the colonists were angry about that.

As a result of the case, James was sentenced to a month in jail, but the Court let Benjamin—who was only 16—get off with a stern warning. To make matters worse, the court also declared that James could no longer run the *New England Courant*, so Benjamin stepped in while his brother was incarcerated. In his own fashion, Benjamin wrote his Silence Dogood pieces and other articles that asserted the colonists' rights to free speech. In one of those Dogood letters, he stated:

> Men ought to speak well of their Governors is true, while their Governors deserve to be well spoken of; but to do public mischief without hearing of it, is only the prerogative and felicity of tyranny: A free people will be showing that they are so, by their freedom of speech.

After James returned, he met with his friends regarding the future of the *New England Courant*. He and they decided to have Benjamin remain on as the new editor, but wanted to draw up a new indenture for him. So, James took back the old indenture and had Benjamin sign a new one for another four years. Soon afterward, Benjamin and James had another dispute, and Ben's father disagreed with Ben this time.

Benjamin didn't want another term of indenture and was growing weary of their frequent bickering, so he permitted his emotions to overcome his judgment and left the print shop without notice. James was incensed and black-balled him all over the area so that Benjamin had difficulty finding new work in Boston. In the British colonies in the 18th century, it was considered a crime to escape one's indenture, so Benjamin's father became enraged about his departure and even put a notice in the *New England Courant* calling for his apprehension and return.

Because his brother had besmirched his reputation in town, Ben decided to go to New York. Surely, he could find work there. With the help of a friend, he sold a lot of his books to finance the journey. In New York, he scouted around for work in the printing business but found none. However, he met a printer named William Bradford who referred him to his son, also a printer, who needed a new employee. Bradford's son worked in Philadelphia, and that meant Franklin would have to travel by sea around the coastline and up the Delaware River. Shortly after he left in a sloop, a storm blew in. After being tossed and turned about, his boat was hung up on some rocks off the coast of Long Island. People tried to help, but nothing could be done until the storm had passed. So, he anchored the boat and tried to sleep. On the following day, he trudged ashore, soaked and filthy. After taking shelter, he grabbed his bag and changed his clothes. The next day, the water was calm, so he sailed for Amboy in New Jersey.

The rest of the journey was made by trudging across acres and acres of land in the incessant rain that haunted him as he crossed New Jersey. Painfully, he had learned that impulsive decisions such as the one that incited him to abandon the security of his print job with James had turned him into a hapless vagabond. He was wet and dirty and must have aroused suspicion among the people who saw him in this sad and sorry state. In his memoirs, he said, "I was thoroughly soaked, and by noon a good deal tired, so I stopped at a poor inn, where I stayed all night beginning now to wish that I had never left home."

Rather than being arrested for being a runaway servant, he discovered the charity of people to whom he was a stranger—and a miserable-looking one at that. The people he met took pity on him. What's more, Franklin discovered the rewards of being friendly and sharing his knowledge with other learned men. At the tavern where he stayed, he befriended the owner, a Dr. Brown. The doctor was fascinated with his superior knowledge, and they conversed many hours. In fact, Franklin maintained that friendship for the rest of his days.

After walking many miles, and paddling rented canoes, 17-year-old Benjamin Franklin arrived in Philadelphia.

Chapter 2 – Naiveté Collides with Reality

In 1723, Franklin pulled up to the Market Street Wharf. It had rained again, and he was soaked and hungry. Ben had only a few pence left and asked a boy to tell him where he might find some bread. After hearing that there was bread at the shop near the shore, he bought what he could for three cents. Again, his friendliness and pitiable innocence appealed to others, and he was given puffy rolls and a lot of copper and silver coins. After buying more bread, he stuffed his pockets with the loaves and strolled along the street munching. A young woman laughed at his comical appearance. She became Franklin's future wife a number of years later.

At long last, he met Andrew, the son of William Bradford, the New York printer who referred him. Unfortunately, Benjamin arrived too late because Bradford had already hired a new apprentice. However, Andrew was generous and offered to introduce him to another in the same trade, but only after he had a tasty breakfast.

His reference, a Mr. Samuel Keimer, was a scholarly man but not an excellent writer. Keimer was the publisher of the *Pennsylvania*

Gazette. He also fancied himself a gifted poet and wanted Franklin to publish some elegies he had composed. Keimer knew nothing about repairing and setting up the old printing press which he had purchased at a discount, so Franklin employed his skills to help him. This was just part-time work, but Bradford offered to board Franklin there in a small room above the shop. It was a dismal room, but served his needs for the time being.

Later on, Andrew Bradford also stopped by, indicating he had occasional need of help at his print shop as well. The printed word barely reached the level of literacy between these two editors. Bradford, unfortunately, was functionally illiterate and Keimer—while somewhat more scholarly—didn't have a feel for journalism. Thus, Franklin survived for a time at these part-time endeavors.

Every once in a while, Benjamin became homesick—in a sense. He had given up living with his family and the securities of home. However, he had been gravely offended by his brother's retributions. Recognizing that he himself bore some responsibility in the private feud and the subsequent abandonment of his own family, he felt both guilt and a sense of pride because he wasn't going to return like the prodigal son. He was determined to be independent and self-sustaining. This was a turning point in his life.

To fight off the feelings of homesickness that crept in on him, Franklin befriended a lot of people in Philadelphia. He was a friendly and lively conversationalist especially at the print shops of Bradford's and Keimer's. When Keimer learned about his homely quarters at Bradford's house, he put Benjamin in touch with the nicer boarding house offered by a Mr. Read. Much to his surprise, Read's daughter was the same young woman who laughed at him with his bread-stuffed pockets wandering the streets. She was a lovely person, and Ben was enamored. He and Deborah dated, and they grew quite fond of each other. As he became more comfortable in his new city, Benjamin met more people there. Discovering that many were educated, Franklin and his new friends engaged in vivacious conversations. As a result of his friendly nature, word traveled, and he was no longer a "stranger" in town. News has a quick way of circulating, and Benjamin's presence became known to the captain of a sloop, Captain Robert Holmes. Coincidentally, Holmes was married to Ben's half-sister, Mary. Holmes regularly sailed a sloop between Boston and Newcastle, which was just south of Philadelphia. He later had a letter delivered to Benjamin, explaining that his family missed him and all would be forgiven if he returned home. Benjamin replied in a carefully worded and discreet letter about his reasons for leaving and his intentions to remain in Philadelphia.

Ben then showed the letter to his brother-in-law, Captain Holmes. Impressed with the composition of the letter, Holmes showed it to his passenger, Sir William Keith, the lieutenant-governor of Pennsylvania. Keith was amazed at the literacy of this young man and commented that the two Philadelphia printers Ben knew were lacking in literary skills. Keith was then determined to help Franklin get a good start in the printing and publishing business by providing him with material to print. Perhaps this would be a stroke of good luck.

The Governor's Surprise Visit

Without notice, Governor Keith and his companion, Colonel French, arrived at Keimer's humble shop. Keimer rushed downstairs to greet them but was astonished when the Governor inquired about Franklin instead of himself. When Franklin came in, Keith complimented him for his skills and suggested that the three of them retire to the local tavern to talk business. Keith had long desired a means by which he could reliably and professionally deliver the news to the colonists about the public businesses of both the governments of Philadelphia and Delaware. Keith then proposed that Benjamin's own father could fund him and set him up in a printing business of his own, where the governor would provide plenty of material to print. Keith promised to give Benjamin a letter to that effect, which would convince Josiah, Ben's father, that the resulting publication would be successful. He then told Franklin to keep this matter private for the time being.

Benjamin's Disappointment

Benjamin made arrangements to go with Captain Holmes to Boston, and the captain eagerly told the Franklin family in advance about his upcoming visit home. By way of a preamble to Benjamin's arrival home, Captain Holmes mentioned to Josiah Franklin that the governor was very impressed with the boy. However, Josiah was a cautious man and asked Holmes many questions about the governor.

Captain Holmes took Benjamin back to Boston and wished him luck. Benjamin arrived at the harbor in a new suit, looking very businesslike and successful. Unlike his arrival in Philadelphia, he now had some silver coins in his pockets and little gifts for his mother and siblings at home. James wasn't there, as he was working at his print shop, and Josiah was out too. Franklin's sisters and mother were delighted when he gave them the gifts. Everyone talked for several hours. They inquired about his well-being and asked him about all of his undertakings since he left. Excitedly, he told them about his experiences in the print shops and his work on the *Pennsylvania Gazette*. His sister, Jane, was particularly delighted to see him, as they had always been very close. In fact, Jane and Benjamin kept up a very close relationship throughout life, and Benjamin was happy to have some time to speak with her.

Franklin then went to visit his brother's printing house. The employees there were very impressed with his fine suit, but James treated Ben in a very curt manner. Benjamin did, however, make it a point to meet with Collins, his dear friend, who was very excited and thrilled to see him. As they talked, Collins entertained the idea of leaving his dreary job at the Boston Post Office and even proposed that he and Benjamin could go to New York to create a new business for themselves that could be more lucrative. Collins was a learned young man, who had studied mathematics and philosophy, and was very interested when Ben talked about his career plans.

Josiah, on the other hand, showed little excitement about the governor's letter, saying that he and Benjamin would discuss it later. When Josiah finally made his opinion known, he told Benjamin that he was pleased the governor took such an interest in his son but felt he was still too young to undertake such a project. Benjamin was just eighteen years old at the time. Josiah then wrote a reply to the governor, indicating he wouldn't fund such an endeavor. Josiah told Benjamin that he might be willing to help set him up in business, but only when he was older and more experienced. Of course, Benjamin was very disappointed.

When he returned to Philadelphia, Franklin heard from Governor Keith again. Keith was dismayed that Josiah Franklin wouldn't help set the boy up in business, so he said,

> Since your father will not set you up, I will do it myself. Give me an inventory of the things necessary to be had from England and I will send for them. You shall repay me when you are able; I am resolved to have a good printer here, and I am sure you will succeed.

Keith then told Franklin to travel to England, and he would give him letters to carry directly to English suppliers. He said he would send a large packet of letters to the ship, several of which would be for Franklin. These, Keith informed him, were letters of credit so that Benjamin could purchase printing equipment and ship it back to Philadelphia. However, the matter must be kept secret, Keith added. On the pretext he was visiting home, Franklin took some time off from the employ of Keimer and Bradford.

Trip to London

Benjamin was scheduled to leave for England in 1724. Before his departure, he proposed to his dear Deborah. However, her mother wouldn't consent to the marriage because he hadn't shown her that he had a visible means of supporting her. The two were crestfallen but agreed to keep in touch. Benjamin felt he could reestablish the relationship when he returned to set up his new print shop.

When he spoke of his upcoming trip to some friends, Benjamin came upon another friend of his, James Ralph, who had also booked passage to London. On board, they met an older gentleman by the name of Thomas Denham, a Quaker merchant. Their friendship was a delightful one, and Denham even had him visit in his spacious cabin aboard ship. When he heard that poor Franklin and Ralph could only afford to travel in steerage, Denham made arrangements for them to stay at a cabin originally intended for his wealthy friend, Andrew Hamilton, who had to cancel at the last moment. What luck!

When he was arriving near the English Channel, Benjamin inquired about the letters that were carried aboard from Governor Keith. The captain, Colonel French, let Benjamin go through his packet of mail in search of Keith's letters for him. There were other letters in the pouch, but none for Franklin...none at all! Benjamin was deeply distressed over that and rushed over to Denham telling him of this. Denham replied he wasn't surprised at all, because he knew that Governor Keith was very unreliable. As for letters of credit, Denham indicated that Keith didn't even have sufficient capital to give anyone a letter of credit. Benjamin was gullible and incredibly naïve, even after having had experiences in life which should have precluded such an occurrence. Denham told Benjamin that he was going to be in Bristol for a while, should he ever have need to visit him, and suggested that Benjamin and his friend look for work in that city where there might be more opportunities.

It was now Christmas Day, 1724, and there they were in London. Ralph had no work prospects there. He was actually deserting his wife, whom he had left in the colonies, and planned on becoming an actor. Now, both were unemployed. When Ralph didn't find an acting job, he moved to Berkshire. So, there was Benjamin going door-to-door at Christmastime in search of work. Much to his surprise, he secured a job at Palmer's small print shop. Palmer didn't publish a newspaper. He published some ads about new stores opening up and printed some material for other customers, so there wouldn't be any opportunities for Franklin to start writing again.

After a year had passed, he secured a better job at Watt's print company, but there was no option there for upward mobility. His friend, James Ralph, also occasionally visited, but mostly for the purpose of borrowing money rather than visiting. Benjamin was generous and always tried to help him out, but Ralph kept it up until Franklin himself was nearly out of money. Benjamin became depressed and was afraid he might have to stay there for the rest of his life.

While he was in London, he made it a point to visit with Thomas Denham from time to time. Two years later, Denham offered Benjamin a job when he returned to Philadelphia. Denham was a merchant and tradesmen in the dry goods business. This wasn't a job in publishing or printing, but Franklin could handle being a bookkeeper, an inventory clerk, and storekeeper if he could move back home. Denham even said he'd be willing to finance Benjamin's trip, and Franklin graciously accepted the offer. They departed for the shores of America and arrived in the summer of 1726. Shortly after he had worked with Thomas Denham, Benjamin developed pleurisy and was sick for some time. As soon as he recovered, however, he returned and assiduously applied himself to his tasks.

Chapter 3 – "B. Franklin, Printer"

Benjamin Franklin liked to sign his writings with the modest credit, "B. Franklin, Printer." When he first started out in Philadelphia, people knew him by that. Even though he had been away for a while, he was still no stranger in town.

When he was back in Philadelphia, he discovered that Deborah Read had married another man in 1725. Unfortunately, her new husband, John Rodgers, greedily grabbed her dowry and disappeared somewhere on the island of Barbados. Because of the bigamy laws, it would be illegal for Franklin to marry Deborah, but it made him heartsick to think that she had been abandoned and was virtually poverty-stricken as a result.

That wasn't the only misfortune of fate to befall him upon his return. Three years later—in 1728—his good friend, Thomas Denham, died of distemper, and his business folded. Franklin was now alone and jobless. There was no one in whom he could confide. These were not good times.

Printing had been his first trade, so he returned to Keimer's print shop. Keimer welcomed him warmly and gave him an even higher position than he originally held. Keimer knew Franklin was experienced in the use of the mechanics of the press and would be a great asset to his business, which had now expanded. Everything there went well until Keimer started arguing with Benjamin frequently. He seemed to find fault with Franklin's work and was often in a bad frame of mind. This reminded Franklin of the abuse of his brother, James, and he became disillusioned, even to the point of questioning his own competence. One day, however, Benjamin discovered that Keimer was heavily in debt. Distraught about this change of circumstance, Benjamin knew that the business might soon fail and was insecure about having to go through the drudgery of finding yet another job. Then, a regular customer came in, a Mr. Hugh Meredith, who was a well-to-do gentleman in Philadelphia. Meredith was in the business of sales and merchandising, and had a constant need of printers. Meredith was also well-aware of Keimer's financial situation and suggested that Franklin go into his own printing business. After Franklin indicated he had no money to do that, Meredith said he would partner with him.

Unlike the unfortunate experience with Governor Keith, Meredith was a responsible man and shipped in equipment from England. Franklin then set it up and hired some men. In 1729, Franklin purchased the *Pennsylvania Gazette* from his former employer, Keimer. Fortunately, Keimer had recovered a little from his financial woes but was still struggling. Keimer had started a new weekly paper, called *Instructor*, but it only had ninety subscribers.

Under Ben Franklin, the *Pennsylvania Gazette* soon became very popular. In order to spice it up a tad, Benjamin published wise adages in it. In addition, he discovered he was a talented advertiser and placed ads in it for Hugh Meredith and other people who wanted to sell goods. He then expanded it to include personal ads but kept certain standards by refusing to print defamatory or libelous articles written by private people. The quality of the print surpassed that of Keimer's paper. In 1730, the colony of New Jersey wanted paper money printed. They compared the quality of the three printers— Bradford, Keimer, and Franklin—and chose Franklin to print the first paper currency in New Jersey. He went to Burlington, New Jersey, with his aide to do that. It was quite a profitable job for Meredith and Franklin, and the extra funds provided capital to widen the circulation of the *Gazette*. After seeing the quality of Franklin's work on the New Jersey currency, Delaware also contracted him to print their money. The fortunes of fate were turning around.

Marriage to Deborah Read

Now that he had met with some success, Benjamin rekindled his relationship with Deborah Read. In 1730, he established a common-law marriage with her. Franklin then acknowledged that he had an illegitimate son, William. Franklin never revealed the identity of William's mother, but Deborah welcomed William into their home anyway and treated him as her own son. They had two more children of their own though, Francis and Sarah.

Deborah was a skillful seamstress and made all of Benjamin's clothes. Years later, he once said, "It was a comfort to me to recollect that I had once been clothed from head to foot in woolen and linen of my wife's manufacture, and that I never was prouder of any dress in my life."

Francis was born in 1732, and they called him "Franky." It is said he was a precocious child and it seemed clear that he was intelligent due to his alertness to all the stimuli around him. Franklin said of him that he was "a golden child, his smiles brighter, his babblings more telling and his tricks more magical than all the other infants in the colonies combined." The smallpox vaccine had been developed by then, but James, Ben's brother, argued against it, believing that it wasn't safe enough. Franklin was in favor of the inoculation, having had one himself. However, Franky was ill for some time with influenza, so he and Deborah delayed, thinking they might wait until he recovered from that. Unfortunately, that took too long, and Francis contracted smallpox. He died in 1736. Benjamin and Deborah were devastated. Following that tragedy, Franklin wrote, "In 1736, I lost one of my sons, a fine boy of four years old, by the smallpox taken in the common way. I long regretted bitterly and still regret it."

The Junto and the First Library

Franklin's relationship with Hugh Meredith became stronger when the two of them started engaging in scholarly conversations. Meredith introduced him to some friends of his—Stephen Potts, George Webb, and a number of others. They had a study club and discussion group which they called "The Leather Apron Club," which was later called the "Junto." Topics were presented in the form of questions, and every time they met, they opined on the subjects. Many of these questions gave Franklin the ability to investigate many areas of science, religion, and politics, which he pursued later on in life.

The Age of Enlightenment, or Age of Reason, was an intellectual movement that arose during the 18th century, which provided the impetus for the Junto. The famous thinkers of that age included John Locke, Isaac Newton, and Voltaire. Thomas Paine and Benjamin Franklin were considered prominent American figures typifying the ideals of that age. The Junto applied logical, philosophical, and scientific approaches to the questions they pondered.

Below are some examples of questions posed at the Junto meetings which Franklin recorded in his diary:

"Can any one particular of government suit all mankind?

"Why does the flame of a candle tend to go upwards in a spire?"

"Should it be the aim of philosophy to eradicate the passions?

"Whence comes the dew that stands on the outside of a tankard that has cold water in it in the summer time?"

"Would not an office of insurance for servants be of service?

The members of the Junto then decided to set up a common library that might benefit others. Franklin organized it and charged a subscription rate. Scholarship in the colonies needed to be encouraged and not all could afford to buy printed books. From the funds, members of the Junto purchased books, and people could go to the building they leased in Philadelphia, as it was open to the general public. The facility was called the "Library Company of Philadelphia." A reader would leave some money down, borrow the book, and the money was returned when the reader returned the book. Lewis Timothy was the first head librarian, and his wife succeeded him in running the library after Peter's death a year later.

His Own Shop

In 1730, Meredith wanted to relocate, so he and Franklin dissolved their partnership under amicable circumstances. Franklin gave him his share of the profits, and Meredith left Benjamin with the ownership of the printing press and equipment. Meredith wanted to establish a company in a Welsh settlement farther south because there were sales opportunities in that area.

By 1731, there were six pages in the bi-weekly *Pennsylvania Gazette*. That was a lot for a newspaper in the early 18th century. It was sold not only in Philadelphia but parts of Delaware as well. Politically, the newspaper took a neutral stance. It contained essays and humorous anecdotes which Franklin himself wrote. One of its distinguishing features was the advertising. Many of the ads had to do with runaway slaves, business, real estate, auctions, and personals. Some were extremely personal, and Franklin eased up on his former principles by printing ads that may have harmed reputations. For example, Mr. Michael McKeel's wife had apparently deserted him, and he wanted to publicly embarrass her and take no responsibility for her:

> Without any just cause of complaint, Mrs. Mary McKeel hath eloped from my bed and board, all persons are therefore desired not to trust her on my account, as I am determined

not to pay any debt she may contract after this date unless she returns to her good behavior. All persons are forewarned, at their peril, (for) harboring her.

Poor Richard's Almanac

Franklin had a great sense of humor and common sense as well. To please the readers' palates, he started publishing *Poor Richard's Almanac* in 1733 and continued publishing it until 1758. The *Almanac* sold about 10,000 copies per year. In addition, he also published the quotations anonymously. Some pithy examples:

1. He's gone, and forgot nothing but to say Farewell to his creditors.

2. He that lies down with dogs, shall rise up with fleas.

3. Better slip with foot than tongue.

4. He that cannot obey, cannot command.

5. Onions can make even heirs and widows weep.

6. Fools make feasts and wise men eat them.

7. A plowman on his legs is higher than a gentleman on his knees.

8. Creditors are a superstitious set, great observers of set days and times.

9. Remember that time is money.

10. God helps them that help themselves.

Franklin initially published *Poor Richard's Almanac* under the pseudonym, "Richard Saunders." In an effort at humor, Franklin falsely foretold the deaths of astrologers of the day. It was in jest, and they understood that.

Later, Franklin changed "Richard Saunders" into "Poor Richard." Poor Richard was based on "Isaac Bickerstaff," a character from Jonathan Swift's writings. Franklin also used *Poor Richard's*

Almanac as a vehicle for his own political philosophy and scientific discussions. Franklin was clever, too. As a teaser, he published many stories in serial form, so he was able to sell the *Almanac* year after year.

Freemasonry

In 1731, Benjamin Franklin joined the Freemasons. Freemasonry is an outgrowth of the Middle Age system of the guilds formed by the cathedral builders and masons. After the Middle Ages were over, the Freemasons found themselves in a membership decline, so they expanded their membership by converting the organization to include social, political, and charitable functions. Freemasonry then became basically a fraternal organization. Members kept the old rituals and symbolism of the 15th century, and it was a secret organization, meaning one would have to apply and may or may not be accepted into a Lodge. Franklin rose quickly into prominence and became a Grand Master in Pennsylvania. In 1734, he edited and reprinted the organization's constitution originally written in 1723.

He also wrote articles about Freemasonry, saying, "I assure you that they are in general a very harmless sort of people, and have no principles or practices that are inconsistent with religion and good manners."

Freemasons take an oath to a set of moral conduct related to the practice of non-sectarianism in religion, obedience to legal, civic authorities, and the application of one's energies toward his respective occupation. Gluttony and drunkenness were forbidden (although members were permitted to drink). Quarreling was discouraged, and members were expected to help each other in times of need—financially and otherwise. Promotion within the society was based solely on merit, not seniority or social status.

Franklin attended the meetings of the Masonic Lodges while he was in England and France in later years. Franklin saw this participation as a means by which he could befriend the nobles and people in those countries, which constituted part of his diplomatic missions.

Chapter 4 – Philosopher, Inventor, and Public Servant

Ideas that were discussed at his Junto meetings planted the seed for new ideas and solutions. Franklin applied his inventive skills toward developing devices and systems that could help everyone in the future. They talked about the most effective plans for recruiting men to the colony militias, along with techniques for fundraising to set up new hospitals, universities, and institutions for the public. One of the topics occasionally discussed at his Junto meetings was the idea of creating a company that could resolve the need for protection for people from the disastrous effects of fire, and at least help them recover after their loss.

The Union Fire Company and Fire Insurance

In 1736, Franklin incorporated the Union Fire Company, modeled after one established in Boston. For a fee, members would join and be required to help other members who might be trapped in their homes; they were also required to furnish six buckets each to the houses belonging to the members. Linen cloths were provided for carrying what goods and valuables they could retrieve from the homes. The service wasn't extended to non-members, however, so more and more fire companies opened up all over Philadelphia to meet the need. Engines with pumps were purchased. Later on, in 1752, a large bell was purchased to be rung in case of fire. In his newspaper, Franklin published articles related to fire prevention. One of the problems he noted was the fact that many people were careless when carrying hot coals from one fireplace to another.

Franklin was also well aware that people lost valuable property due to fire and suffered financially because of that. To answer the need, Franklin set up the country's first insurance company, called The Philadelphia Contributionship for the Insuring of Houses from Loss by Fire. It was incorporated in 1753, and Franklin was named "The Father of American Insurance." During its first year, the company wrote policies for 143 members.

The American Philosophical Society

In 1743, Franklin founded the American Philosophical Society. It was an outgrowth of his fondness for the Junto group that he and a number of friends established to discuss questions about nature and beliefs about morals, natural phenomena, and physics. A friend of his in Philadelphia was a botanist and talked to Franklin about setting up a society that could ponder scientific and philosophical issues and write about them. Some of the themes they discussed were farm production, grain importation, mining techniques, mapmaking, the study of fossils, and mapmaking.

This society remains active, but its membership fell off during the 1760s. At that time, it was reinvigorated by Charles Tomson, who altered the themes to include medicine, chemistry, trade, commerce, and other pursuits.

Retirement from Printing

Franklin's interest in inventing and science was growing so he reassessed his financial situation and his print shops, which were now well-established. There were shops not only in Philadelphia and its environs but in New York and the West Indies. He also contemplated one in Jamaica that he hoped two of his nephews would run. His plan for his nephews required six-year apprenticeships under a journeyman Franklin would hire. If the businesses did well, his nephews could buy the press and continue on their own. That way, they could support themselves.

David Hall was his journeyman at his main shop. Hall was very skilled, and Franklin implicitly trusted him. In 1748, Franklin made Hall a partner, and drew up a contract by which Hall would have full use of the equipment and Franklin would receive a regular payment. This contract called for Franklin to receive a portion of the profits for about twenty years.

The Franklin Whale-Oil Lamp

In the very early days of colonial America, the settlers used what was called the "Betty Lamp." The earliest versions used animal fat that was melted and poured into a metal canister with a wick in it, after which it cooled and hardened. The canister was held up by a hook, and the people would light the wick, which would burn like a candle emitting light. The Betty lamp could then be carried from room to room in order to see at night. Later on, whale oil or fish oil could be used which gave better light.

In 1740, there were some improvements on that model, one of which was invented by Benjamin Franklin. It consisted of two wick tubes spaced just one tube-space apart. It was discovered that Franklin's lamp gave off three times as much light as the other one and even the two-wick models developed before that. In the 1860s, Abraham Lincoln used the Franklin version of the lamp in his Illinois law office.

The Franklin Stove

In 1742, Ben Franklin noted, "It is strange, methinks, that though chimneys have been for so long in use, the construction should be so little understood till lately that no workman pretended to make one

26

which would carry off the smoke." He also complained that traditional fireplaces drew cold air into the room and sometimes the cold air hit one's back while keeping the front of them warm. He then designed a stove, the function of which was to radiate heat. His first stove consisted of iron sides and a top and back with an opening in the front, like a fireplace. The stovepipe was exposed until it joined the chimney, which would help radiate heat. He called his first invention "The Pennsylvania Stove." He later improved it by adding a hollow baffle that acted as a reverse siphon, drawing some of the excess loss of heat downwards to add to the temperature. It didn't sell that well, as he had made an error in the placement of the flue. Much later, a scientist, David Rittenhouse, solved that problem, but the credit for the idea was Franklin's.

Franklin's Electrostatic Machine

Since he was a child, Franklin noticed static electricity, which is when a spark flies out from a person's finger after they rub it on a piece of wool or something similar. He wanted to explore the concept further, so he attended some lectures by Ebenezer Kinnersley in Philadelphia. Franklin then purchased Kinnersley's equipment and took it home for further experimentation. Many of the electrical experiments performed at the time utilized a glass tube for the generation of electrical charges. Franklin increased the intensity of these charges by rotating a glass globe instead, which was rotated by hand with a crank. At the base of the sphere, he mounted a swatch of leather on which it would rub with every turn. Just outside the globe, he positioned vertical metal needles. As the globe turned, sparks flew out and made contact with the needles, creating a mini-bolt. Franklin called this "electrical fire," and published a paper on it called "Electrical Minutes," which has since been lost.

Using a beaded iron chain, Franklin collected the electricity generated and fed it into a Leyden jar. The early Leyden jars were glass bottles lined with thin metal, and each contained a metal rod attached to it leading upwards. The Leyden jar is an early version of a capacitor, which stores potential electricity. The final outcome was the 18th-century version of a battery. Franklin sensed that, if he combined the principles demonstrated in these experiments, he could develop a practical use for it.

Despite the success of this invention, there was still superstition among some people. A Boston minister called Franklin a blasphemous meddler by "tampering with the battery of heaven!"

Invention of the Lightning Rod

Franklin was aware of the dangers of coming into direct contact with a lightning bolt. He also understood the concept of insulators which wouldn't conduct electricity and preserve one from being electrocuted. In 1751, he constructed a silk kite, as paper could easily be burned by a lightning strike. The current would be conducted through the twine tied to the kite. The lower part of the twine was held inside so as to remain dry because water conducts electricity. To that twine, Franklin attached a key. Then he and his son, William, went out during a thunderstorm and flew the kite into a storm cloud. When a bolt hit it, Franklin noticed that the bristles of the twine hemp stood on end. As he moved his finger very close to the key, a spark flew. From what he learned from his kite experiments, he designed the first lightning rod.

Success in any scientific endeavor depends upon the universality of the concepts and formulas theorized, and as scientists were able to duplicate these experiments, they approved of the usefulness of the lightning rod, and many were manufactured. Some of the less enlightened preachers of the day mocked his kite experiments and said Franklin was "flying in the face of Providence."

The Single Fluid Theory

From his experiments with electricity, Franklin theorized that electricity flowed from a single "fluid," which would explain its passage from one person or conductive object to another. He recognized the charges as being positive or negative. The current runs from the positive to the negative charge such as what happens in a battery.

In 1753, Franklin was awarded the Copley Medal from the Royal Society of London for his "curious experiments and observations on electricity." Later on, in 1759, the University of St. Andrews awarded him *in absentia* with an honorary degree of Doctor of Laws. It was said that Professors David Gregory, David Young, and/or Thomas Simson might have made the proposal that he be so honored. In 1762, Oxford University also gave him an honorary doctoral degree for his contributions to science.

The Bifocal Lens

Although Franklin didn't even complete college, he constantly queried about everyday items with a view to improve them. He was what one might call an "idea man." Franklin found it annoying to constantly change his spectacles, as he had to use one pair to look ahead and the other to read. To resolve the nuisance of switching frequently from one to the other, he had bifocals made. The optometrist, John Isaac Hawkins, inventor of the trifocal lens, credited Ben Franklin with the invention of bifocal glasses, and publicized it. He knew Franklin was a humble man, but Hawkins wanted him to receive credit for it, as it was well-deserved.

Academy and College of Philadelphia

Back in 1739, Benjamin Franklin came across an Anglican preacher by the name of George Whitefield. He wanted to open what he called a "charity school" in Georgia and traveled to some of the colonies conducting revivalist meetings. Rev. Whitefield held some of these revivalist meetings in Philadelphia to raise funds for his proposed charity school. Franklin's wife attended one meeting and encouraged Franklin to do so as well. Franklin went and was impressed with Rev. Whitefield's powerful voice and speaking style. About his speaking style, Franklin said:

His delivery of the sermon was so improved by frequent repetition that every accent, every emphasis, every modulation of voice, was so perfectly well turned and well placed that without being interested, I, the subject, could not help being pleased with the discourse.

Although Franklin wasn't an Anglican, he became friends with this itinerant preacher and helped him build an establishment in Philadelphia. Franklin and Whitefield had jocular debates, and the preacher often tried to convert Franklin. Franklin, on the other hand, encouraged Whitefield to include a larger primary school as well. To help in fundraising, Franklin even printed some of his sermons. Franklin felt that preachers of any religious persuasion should be allowed to preach in Pennsylvania and around the country. The school was built, but due to Whitefield's increasing popularity, it needed to be expanded. Franklin then proposed that more subjects be added and a larger school be established.

In 1749, Franklin and some other notables talked about including a more advanced curriculum and the addition of a secondary school. Many schools at the time followed the English model and taught Anglicanism to the exclusion of other religions. During his upbringing, Franklin was taught Presbyterianism based on the dogmas of John Calvin. He rebelled against that when older, and likewise wasn't heavily committed to Anglicanism, although he didn't reject it either. He was a Deist, as he believed in God as a creator who occasionally intervened in the world and aided mankind. He did believe in prayer and once said, "Without the belief of a Providence that takes cognizance of, guards and guides, and may favor particular persons, there is no motive to worship or fear its displeasure, or to pray for its protection." Franklin was impatient with religious debates because he felt that no one could have a full comprehension of a divinity that is unseen but only can be understood in terms of creation. He felt that religion was important because it was needed to prevent people from becoming wicked. However, he didn't see the value in enforcing one particular religion over another. Through his experiences in Pennsylvania, he developed an admiration for Quakers and ministers whom he came to admire. He disagreed with other ministers, not in terms of their beliefs, but because of their vigorous evangelism. Franklin therefore insisted that the school be non-sectarian. He said,

> Both the house and ground were vested in trustees, expressly for the use of any preacher of any religious persuasion who might desire to say something to the people at Philadelphia; the design in building not being to accommodate any particular sect, but the inhabitants in general; so that even if the Mufti of Constantinople were to send a missionary to preach Mohammedanism to us, he would find a pulpit at his service.

A new building was proposed and partially planned, but Rev. Whitefield, who really preferred to be an itinerant preacher, returned to the South. In 1751, Franklin and a few notables in the area aspired to create a college. Franklin then selected Rev. William Smith to be the provost. Fortunately, Smith agreed with Franklin's non-sectarian approach, so that made it easier. Franklin also preferred that the sciences be taught along with the classics and mathematics, instead of Greek and Latin. This institution focused on preparing students for business, rather than for the clergy like the traditional universities: Yale, Harvard, William and Mary College, and Princeton. Later on, in 1755, it was granted a charter and became the College of Philadelphia. After the American Revolution started, the college became a hotbed of politics, and a plethora of Loyalist pamphlets was issued from there. In 1779, the colonial government took it over. This upset Franklin, who had intended the college to be an institution of learning, not an organ of politics. After the war was over, it was reopened. The college was re-chartered, and a year after Franklin's death, it became the prestigious University of Pennsylvania, as it is known today.

From Clerk to Delegate

Since 1736, Franklin had been serving as a clerk to the Philadelphia City Council under Patrick Gordon, the deputy governor. In 1753, Franklin was elected to the Pennsylvania Assembly and was also appointed Postmaster General of the British colonies by England. The postal service prior to that only used older horses, and mail delivery was usually very slow. He introduced the use of a "stage wagon," which could carry more mail and move faster because there was a team of horses pulling it. He then introduced a "fast-mail" service that promised quicker delivery. It was remarkably successful, especially because a lot of business was conducted that way.

On the following year, seven of the British colonies—Maryland, Connecticut, New Hampshire, Massachusetts, New York, Rhode Island, and Pennsylvania—held a meeting at Albany, New York. It seems the French were willfully building forts in Pennsylvania and New York. Borders of these colonies had been established earlier, and the British colonies were becoming concerned about this intrusion. In addition, the French were making strides in allying themselves with some of the tribes in those regions, mostly those known to the French fur trappers who had been living and working in those areas for years before. One of the purposes of the Albany conference was to cement an alliance with the Iroquois nation, also known as the Six Nations. These tribes were also asked to send representatives to the Albany meeting. To this day, the Six Nations still exists as a united confederation whose headquarters is on the Native American territory of the Onondaga tribe (south of the city of Syracuse).

The other purpose for the Albany meeting was presented by Benjamin Franklin and was called the "Plan of Union." This plan called for the levying of taxes to finance any possible hostile actions and for the defense in this contested region. It was passed by the colonial delegates but wasn't approved by the English authorities, who were anxious that the colonists be prevented from the right to levy taxes.

Political Life and Foreign Affairs

In 1754, the French and Indian War broke out. It took place mostly in northern Pennsylvania, which was part of the Ohio River Valley. Troops were led by General Edward Braddock. George Washington, a colonel and later the first president of the United States, was one of the commanders of that expedition.

Franklin worked for the Philadelphia Militia by helping to create a system to finance Pennsylvania's portion of the expenses for carriages, horses, and food for the soldiers who were serving in the French and Indian War. Many of his meetings were held at the Tun Tavern in Philadelphia. Franklin frequented the tavern from which he made a number of recruitment efforts. This tavern became the birthplace of the Marines, which was first authorized in 1775, and it served as a base for recruitment for the new Continental Army during the American Revolution. A replica of the tavern exists at the Marine base in Quantico, Virginia.

Chapter 5 – Benjamin Franklin: England 1757-1762

Ben Franklin, the Penn Family, and Great Britain

As heirs, the Penn family owned a great deal of territory in Pennsylvania by virtue of a land grant by Charles II. They arbitrarily announced that they weren't responsible for any taxes at all and overturned the colonial legislation requiring them to do so. That meant that very little money was going into the treasury of Pennsylvania. The colony also needed the money to defend its unsettled regions. Because the monies collected from Pennsylvania wouldn't be sufficient in the short-term, the Assembly proposed a twelve-year plan to pay for it. Deputy governor Robert Morris refused to sign it, insisting upon a term of five years. It was impossible for Pennsylvania to meet that goal.

The contentious issue went back and forth between the governor and the assembly. William Penn's son then appointed William Denny as the new deputy governor. Because of a last-minute proposal with Deputy Governor William Denny, a ten-year property tax by the Pennsylvania Assembly included the Penn properties. Denny refused to sign that. To appeal the matter, Ben Franklin himself wrote to the very influential English lord, Robert Charles, complaining about it. There was no response. As a result, the colonists and Denny came to a less than ideal agreement, so the funds were exhausted rapidly. Now, more funds were needed.

In 1757, in his capacity as a delegate to the Pennsylvania Assembly, Benjamin Franklin was asked to go to London to represent the colonists of Pennsylvania against the overwhelming power of William Penn's descendants. Franklin arrived in London and took his son, William, with him.

First of all, Benjamin Franklin met with the hostility of some of the British noblemen including Thomas Fermor, the Earl of Pomfret. William Penn's son, Thomas, had married Fermor's daughter and together they lived in Pennsylvania. However, Thomas Penn was in England at that time, along with his younger brother Richard. Franklin contacted them there with regard to the grievances of the Pennsylvania colony. Penn, of course, was adamantly opposed to Franklin's entreaty, even though Franklin brought up the issue of the hardships it would create if he opposed. Instead of addressing the matter with Franklin directly, Thomas Penn sent Franklin's letter to the King's Council, noting that Franklin wasn't respectful because he hadn't used the proper salutation mentioning Penn's official titles. Franklin intended his missive to be an informal request, though, but Penn chose to overlook that. The matter dragged on unresolved for months. John Paris, Penn's attorney and solicitor general, was handling the case and he delayed his work on it. Finally, Paris completed his phase of the case and forwarded it to the attorney general, Charles Pratt. Pratt repudiated Franklin's appeal. However, the matter still needed to be reviewed by the Privy Council so there might still be a chance.

To tarnish Franklin's reputation, Thomas Penn also sent a haughty letter to the Pennsylvania Assembly saying that Franklin lacked candor and was disrespectful. Penn's attorney then followed up with a similar letter. In defense of Franklin, two members of the

Pennsylvania Assembly spoke up and called the actions of the Penn family tyrannical.

While he was awaiting the ruling from the Privy Council, Franklin used the time to establish amicable relations with other English officials. His friendly manner and cordiality resulted in good contacts there that could be used in the future to improve the relations between England and the colonists. Franklin made the acquaintance of Lord Bute, the prime minister, and prevailed upon him to appoint his son, William Franklin, to the governorship of New Jersey. Other notables in England he contacted included Dr. Joseph Priestley, physicist and philosopher; Richard Jackson, the counsel for the Trade Commission; Dr. Joseph Hadley, scientist; Lord Kames, a Scottish lawyer, judge, and philosopher; and William Strahan, a member of Parliament. Franklin took this opportunity and sent Kames his 1755 publication on population studies because it had political implications. The publication had already been republished in England and was a topic of discussion by politicians and philosophers as well.

While Franklin was waiting, he continually made contacts within the English government. He also spoke with many of the British about the colonies and conversed with interested parties about his own writings.

Population Studies

Intellectuals in Great Britain asked Franklin about his study on population, which was called "Observations Concerning the Increase of Mankind." Some were distressed because of the increase in population growth in the colonies and feared that the American population might soon be larger than that in England. If the population in the colonies was to surpass that of Britain, they thought it might be necessary to place restrictions upon British America so it could still be controlled. Addressing those concerns, Franklin pointed out that population growth could be a boon for Great Britain because of the increase in trade. He presented solid rationale for his premise in terms of the vast amount of unsettled land available. That land, he indicated, could be used to construct manufacturing plants and expand farming, plantations, and animal husbandry. He stated, "Land being thus plenty in America, and so cheap that a laboring man who understands husbandry can in a short time save money enough to purchase a piece of new land sufficient for a plantation." He went on further to say that it will take many ages to fully settle the land and would represent new opportunities for a long time.

When England annexed Quebec, Franklin also registered his approval because the population of British America would be increased and help make both the colonies and Quebec stronger on the world stage. He wrote to Lord Kames in 1760 saying, "I have long been of the opinion that the foundations of the future grandeur and stability of the British Empire lie in America," and commented that he needed to append his publication on population growth due to the British annexation of Quebec.

Benjamin Franklin and Joseph Priestley

Both Dr. Joseph Priestley and Ben Franklin studied the politics of England firsthand and came to the realization that King George III and his immediate advisors were feeding into English hostility toward the colonies. Priestley was a supporter of equal rights and religious tolerance, as well as a noted scientist.

As they spoke with each other, Franklin found out that Priestley was experimenting with electricity and gases. Franklin then collaborated with Priestley in the writing of his essay, "History and Present State of Electricity." First, Franklin and Priestley duplicated an experiment with gases attributed to the chemist, Antoine Lavoisier. Franklin worked with Priestley and varied the procedure, which led to the discovery of a substance they called "dephlogisticated air." Priestley and Franklin applied it to the biological process of promoting better respiration. Priestley later improved the procedure and is credited with the discovery and isolation of oxygen as a pure element.

Benjamin Franklin and Dr. John Hadley

In 1758, when he visited Cambridge University, Franklin contacted Dr. John Hadley, a professor of chemistry. Together they conducted experiments by dipping a thermometer into a vial of ether and discovered that, when they removed it, the thermometer dropped several degrees. They repeated this over and over again until finally the thermometer registered a temperature that was below freezing. The both of them then concluded that evaporation was a useful tool to cool an object down. Franklin later said that a man could freeze to death on a summer day by applying this principle. This is an innovation later used to make air conditioners.

While he was studying this, Franklin also observed that black clothing is warmer than white clothing in the summer heat. However, he didn't delineate the property of the pigments which contributes to that effect.

Benjamin Franklin was constantly alert to phenomena around him, even the most trivial. On occasion, he would develop a new invention, and at other times, propose a series of questions for scientists and thinkers to ponder and answer. About eight years prior to his arrival in England, Franklin reflected on the function of sweat on the human body and noted that it cooled his body to some extent. At that time, he noted that sweat was essential to protecting a human being during excessively hot weather, but the essential benefits of sweat weren't long-lasting. He then discovered that adding some diluted liquor to water and applying it to the body slowed the cooling effect so that it lasted longer.

Invention of the New Odometer

Franklin was forever thinking and developing mechanical solutions for everyday situations. In 1760, in England, the British tapped into his illustrious mind regarding ways to make postal delivery systems more efficient. The odometer came into being in ancient times, but it wasn't that precise in its measurements. While at home, Franklin had toyed with many ideas as to how to create one that was more accurate. He compared the distances traveled with how many revolutions a wagon wheel would make to reach one mile. He discovered that the wheel would make 400 revolutions to cover a distance of one mile, or 1.6 kilometers, and suggested that the English work on a device that could use that data.

Invention of the Armonica

In 1761, Franklin watched a demonstration of the glass harmonica in Cambridge. He then improved on the design and invented a more mechanical apparatus to yield clearer tones from the glass structure. He worked with a London glassblower, Charles James, to build it. Because it used a keyboard, variations in the sound could be made. Franklin's version used 37 glass bowls and chords that could be played—an impossibility with the original design. This instrument Franklin called the "Armonica." Franz Mesmer, who developed the technique of hypnosis called "mesmerism" in the later 18th century, used Franklin's Armonica as an integral part of his procedure. Beethoven also used it to produce his melodrama, *Leonore Prohaska*. A replica of the instrument has been utilized by the current performing dance company, the Joffrey Ballet.

Ruling of the Privy Council

After waiting for so long, Franklin received the ruling of the Privy Council on his presentations regarding the collection of taxes from the Penn family. In their ruling, the Privy Council stated that Pennsylvania had the right to charge and collect taxes from the Penn family. However, there were a lot of caveats to that which diluted that right in the form of six amendments. The colonists were furious and refused to sign the amendments. Deputy Governor Hamilton, the new governor of Pennsylvania, had been in league with Thomas Penn and continued to pressure the Assembly in Pennsylvania to sign the amendments, but they would only sign a few.

Pennsylvania's Reaction

In the colonies, Franklin's political enemies made fodder of his failure. A cartoon even appeared in a circulation that had a caricature of the devil with Franklin saying, "Thee shall be my agent, Ben, for all my dominions."

It should be pointed out that many of those people had connections to the Penn family, who spread their hostility far and wide. Even though some of the Pennsylvanians were irate about Franklin's less than stellar performance, the Pennsylvania Assembly considered it at least mildly successful because Pennsylvania was able to levy some taxes on the Penn family properties. Nevertheless, because Pennsylvania didn't want to continue to pay Franklin a salary, they called him home. Franklin himself also knew he had a lot of work to do with the Assembly in terms of dealing with England. In 1762, he arrived in Philadelphia. Much to his shock, Franklin witnessed angry mobs from all over the colonies, and many people were hostile toward him.

To make an attempt at amends, he turned over his earned salary of $15,000 back to the colony. He still felt, though, that it would be in Pennsylvania's best interest to continue working on a positive relationship with England.

Chapter 6 – Benjamin Franklin in London: 1764-1769

In 1764, Great Britain passed a tax on sugar. Many of the taxes were hardships for the colonists who had already raised a great deal of money to supply the troops during the French and Indian War. In addition, the farmers experienced some downturns in their profits due to the weather. The colonists also underwent a crisis because gold and silver became scarce. Landowners and others had the resources, but without the precious metals, they were unable to conduct business. To resolve the problem, the colonies issued their own currency called "Bills of Credit," but there was an uneven system for providing security to back up the bills. Some banks based it on the value of land alone. Other banks charged interest, but some didn't. Certain "Bills of Credit" were only targeted to pay a debt, but not for buying and selling.

British merchants were also very uneasy about accepting the new unstandardized paper currency. So, in 1764, Parliament passed the Currency Act which prohibited the colonies from issuing their own paper currency and presented them with one-pound British notes to use. This created confusion. As a result of this new act, the British government was controlling currency in the colonies, and there was an uproar. The Pennsylvania Assembly then quickly sent Franklin to England again. The colonies of New Jersey, Georgia, and Massachusetts also appointed him as their agent in London. They recognized that Franklin was a successful businessman in his own right, and that was an important asset.

Financial Burdens on the Colonies

Shortly after his arrival, Franklin contacted influential figures in England. Regarding the Sugar Act and Currency Act, he spoke to Richard Jackson of the House of Commons, whom he had met on his earlier trip. Jackson was in charge of trade and commodities in England. Franklin told Jackson that the sugar came from the British West Indies and shouldn't be taxed as a British product. In addition, he intimated that America might resort to buying sugar from Native Americans who could grow it in and near the Spanish territories in Florida. Franklin also presented a case for allowing the colonists to trade lumber and iron directly with Ireland.

The Stamp Act of 1765

In 1765, the Stamp Act was passed. It wasn't a tax on stamps, per se; it was a tax on the embossed paper the colonists needed to draw up legal papers, newspapers, and the like. Franklin voiced his opposition to it on the basis that the British colonies had no representation in the English Parliament and mentioned that to Jackson as well. Franklin also wanted to contact Lord Bute, who was the prime minister in England during Franklin's last visit, but, unfortunately, Bute had been replaced by George Grenville. Grenville usually catered to the whims of the king. Because of the attitudes of the new prime minister, he was unable to make any headway. Franklin then continually tried to meet with Parliament. He was well-versed and versatile, and used his interpersonal skills to glean influence in the political sphere. One gentleman, by the name of William Strahan, was a printer Franklin met twenty years ago. During this visit, he and Strahan often chatted about print styles, formats, and fonts. When Strahan was elected to Parliament, Franklin was thrilled because he needed supporters there. Strahan made attempts on behalf of Franklin but had little success getting a hearing because Prime Minister Grenville continued to defend the tax strenuously. Franklin soon concluded that the passage of the Stamp Act was inevitable. In a letter to a friend just a few weeks later, Franklin wrote, "We might as well have hindered the sun setting."

In 1765, Franklin's wife wrote to him, saying that she and the children had to flee to Burlington, New Jersey in order to escape the wrath of the mobs who were harassing them in Philadelphia. People blamed Franklin for the failure to get the Stamp Act repealed. In the streets, more protests erupted. A secret organization, the Sons of Liberty, formed in Massachusetts to devise methods to fight taxation. Prominent members were Samuel Adams, Patrick Henry, and two of Franklin's fellow Pennsylvanian statesmen, John Hancock and Paul Revere. The situation was becoming dire.

The Quartering Act of 1765

Great Britain then passed the Quartering Act, which required that the colonists financially provide for the housing of British soldiers in the colonies who couldn't secure rooms in colonial rooming houses and hotels. That meant that barns, stables, taverns, and storehouses belonging to the colonists had to be used to house these soldiers. This was an intrusion on the privacy of the colonists and effectively substituted for another tax by requiring them to pay for this housing. Even Prime Minister Grenville was somewhat uncomfortable about it. Franklin took advantage of that and worked out a compromise by communicating with his friend, Thomas Pownall of Massachusetts. The both of them developed the Pownall-Franklin Compromise, which denied entry onto private property but provided housing in empty buildings and had the colonial governments foot the costs of some basic provisions for the soldiers. Grenville approved of this and signed the compromise. While the colonists objected to the

Quartering Act, the impetus of their protests turned back to the hated Stamp Act. In fact, the colonists started finding clever ways of avoiding it by using old paper and even smuggling some paper from willing merchants. As these actions increased, England's profit from the Stamp Act decreased substantially. As a result, England started sending over more British troops in order to attempt to enforce the act, but that wasn't successful. British officials were harassed on the streets and at their offices, with some vandalism occurring as well.

Rotating Prime Ministers

Grenville developed personal disputes with King George because he was forced to reduce the personal allowance for the king, who was an extravagant spender. The king had also been subject to a barrage of complaints from the colonies and was pummeled with letters from the more influential colonists who said that they needed representation in the English Parliament. In 1765, the king dismissed Grenville from office and replaced him with Charles, the Marquess of Rockingham. Rockingham was much more interested in horse racing than in the ministry and lasted only thirteen months! William Pitt "The Elder" replaced him. Pitt was more sympathetic to the American cause, and the king hoped that Pitt could resolve the matter peaceably. Pitt, however, was getting very ill and appointed Charles Townshend, the exchequer, to step into his role. Because of his accounting skills, Townshend realized that the English war debt from the Seven Years' War was depleting the treasury of England and looked toward the colonies as a fresh source of revenue. In 1767, he persuaded Parliament to pass the Townshend Acts which was a series of five taxes in the form of import taxes, excise taxes, and the like. Knowing that America had been starting to manufacture its own goods, Townshend selected items he suspected the colonies couldn't easily manufacture like lead, paint, china, and glass, taxing those as well. Then Townshend suddenly died. William Pitt had, by then, become so ill that he had to retire from office and was succeeded by Augustus Fitzroy, the Duke of Grafton, who preferred to humor the king rather than get the job done. He served as prime minister for two years and was succeeded by Frederick Lord North in 1770. Franklin had a good relationship with William Pitt, but all of the others were Tories or under the thumb of the king and supported the excessive taxation.

This excessive taxation forced the colonists to initiate a boycott against British goods. "Save your money and save your country" was the popular slogan the Patriots used to fuel their campaign.

The American Boycott and Repeal of the Stamp Act

Ben Franklin wasted no time and spread the word around England that the colonies would manufacture their own goods and boycott English imports. Even though some items were difficult to manufacture in the colonies, a boycott would still have a heavy impact on trade. Patriots in the colonies also vandalized some of the retail stores selling British products. As this protest continued, the English merchants complained bitterly. The British government wasn't able to collect taxes on their exports that remained unsold. The king himself soon realized that his trade with the colonies was being affected. In addition, the Whig Party in England lent some support to the American cause. The Marquess of Rockingham, who served just a short time as prime minister, supported the repeal of the Stamp Act in particular, although he did nothing about it while in office. The powerful political philosopher and orator, Edmund Burke, understood the motive behind the boycott, and eloquently spoke up about the injustice.

In 1766, the House of Commons asked Franklin to appear to answer questions concerning the Stamp Act, other taxes, and the boycott. They asked, "Are not all the people very able to pay those taxes?" Franklin replied, "No. The frontier counties, all along the continent, having been frequently ravaged by the enemy (Native American tribes) and greatly impoverished. They are able to pay very little tax." The term "frontier" referred to large rural areas such as western Pennsylvania, New York, southern New Jersey, and other outlying districts.

When asked, "Do you think it right that America should be protected by this country and pay no part of the expense?" he answered, "That is not the case. The colonies raised, clothed and paid during the last war (the Seven Years' War), provided near twenty-five thousand men and spent many millions." The British had promised to reimburse the colonists for such expenditures, so they asked Franklin about that. Franklin responded to that concern by saying that the British reimbursement to the colonies amounted to only 40% of their expenses. He also added that the colonies had no representation in Parliament so they couldn't vote on the laws that affected them.

The House of Commons then directly addressed the issue brought up by Franklin himself related to his population studies. They asked how much the population of America had increased since it became British America. He said,

> I think the inhabitants of all the provinces together, taken at a medium, will double in about twenty-five years. But their demand for British manufactures will increase much faster…but (only) grows with the growing abilities of the same numbers to pay for them.

That clever answer informed the British that it would be to their advantage if they made concessions. Franklin also dovetailed into that response the implication that high taxes would only serve to reduce the colonists' ability to pay for goods sent from Great Britain.

During his appearance, Franklin also addressed the hardships caused by the Currency Act of 1764. He told Richard Jackson of the Trade Commission that the Currency Act would cause the colonists to hoard what legal tender they already had. When asked about the colonists' attitudes toward Parliament, he said they no longer had much respect for Parliament because of its severe restrictions related to currency.

One of the most repeated questions had to do with the quality of British goods. Franklin politely answered that British goods were of excellent quality, but the colonists were now making their own clothes and goods and would continue to do so if the excessive taxes continued to be levied. Franklin was amazingly calm when he said that, making it a point to omit any hostile statements, although he must have felt that way.

The House then presented Franklin with the key question, "Do you not think the people of America would submit to pay the stamp duty, if it was moderated?" Franklin firmly responded, "No, never, unless compelled by force of arms."

William Pitt, who was now serving in the House of Commons after his prolonged illness, asserted England's right to tax the colonists but felt that the difficulties imposed by the Stamp Act were far too burdensome. He had a strong voice in the House, and his address helped Franklin a great deal. He said that "…the Stamp Act should be repealed absolutely, totally and immediately; that the reason for the repeal…was founded on an erroneous principle." He also likened it to "taking money out of the colonists' pockets without their consent."

Edmund Burke said of Franklin's appearance, "Dr. Franklin, as he stood before the bar of Parliament, presented such an aspect of dignity and intellectual superiority as to remind me of a schoolmaster questioned by schoolboys." In 1766, the notorious Stamp Act was repealed. The highest tribute came from the lips of King George himself when he uttered, "That crafty American is more than a match for you all!"

News traveled rapidly in the colonies. Astonishingly, even Lieutenant-Governor Penn entertained several hundred distinctive guests in the state house, and they all drank to the health of Dr. Franklin. A banquet was held in his honor on a barge named "Franklin" in the Schuylkill River. After that, the merchants from the colonies of Georgia, Massachusetts, and New Jersey appointed him as their agent in London, and he was paid handsomely to serve in that capacity. However, in Massachusetts, there was opposition to his appointment by the eminent politician, Samuel Adams. Adams felt that Ben Franklin was well-meaning but too passionate and easy-going. Franklin always spoke in a calm and rational manner, but Adams had been raised in a very restricted puritanical household and was much more reserved than Franklin.

The Townshend Acts

In 1767, Great Britain had passed the Townshend Acts that imposed excise taxes on items exported to the colonies, including glass, paper, and tea. It even required that shipments made from other European countries go to England first and be taxed before being forwarded to America. John Dickinson, a colonial patriot, had his "Farmer's Letters" published in the colonies in 1767 to protest the Townshend Acts. He sent a copy to Ben Franklin, who added a preface to the piece and had it published not only in England but in Ireland and France as well.

Franklin also fought back in the most powerful of media—the printed word. He masqueraded as an anonymous Englishman and published letters under various pseudonyms in the *London Chronicle* and other widely-read publications in England. He interspersed his remarks with wit and a sense of humor. This attracted a wide readership, and some of his letters were even republished in Paris.

Franklin Alters His Opinion

Up until that point, Ben Franklin had been lobbying for a compromise between Great Britain and the colonies, as he felt that the English were intelligent men and could be reasonable, given a little persuasion. However, he witnessed first-hand the hostility and close-mindedness in Great Britain. He was confronted by the stubbornness of the prime ministers, with the exception of William Pitt. They had overwhelming power over King George III and the House of Burgesses in Parliament. The colonists' angry reactions, which Franklin knew were justified, was rising to a fever pitch. He then started to reverse his opinion about England. Every time America forged a compromise about legislation passed in England, another tax or burden was imposed. The relationship between America and England was deteriorating. Events happened with alarming rapidity. Franklin observed, "Things daily wear a worse aspect, and tend more and more to a breach and final separation."

Chapter 7 – Benjamin Franklin in London: 1769-1775

Repeal of the Townshend Acts

In 1769, British trade with America was half that of 1768. What's more, many of the colonies united in their efforts to resist the taxes on British goods. Some British vessels were even turned back from American ports. The merchants in England formed an association and complained incessantly to Parliament and the new prime minister, Lord North. The merchants even resorted to trickery to get their goods sold in America but met with little success. Finally, in 1770, Lord North and Parliament repealed all but one of the Townshend Acts because of Franklin's efforts. The one remaining act was the tax on tea.

The *Craven Street Gazette*

In 1770, Franklin purchased a printing press and started his own publication in London called the *Craven Street Gazette*. In terms of politics, Franklin responded to his newspaper correspondents. In one letter to a prominent businessman of England, he said:

I see with pleasure, that we think pretty much alike on the subject of English America. We of the colonies have never insisted that we ought to be exempt from contributing to the common expenses necessary to support the prosperity of the empire. We only assert that, having parliaments (assemblies) of our own, and not having representatives in that of Great Britain, our parliaments are the only judges of what we can and what we ought to contribute in this case; and that the English Parliament has no right to take our money without our consent.

One of the intents of the *Craven Street Gazette* was also to create a release for Franklin's penchant for light sarcasm and humor as well as political issues. An article he published in 1770 was a fictional piece about the depressing effects of the absence of Queen Margaret on the population when she was away and the mischief it caused. In the article, he wrote, "It is remarked that the skies have wept every day in Craven Street because of the absence of the Queen." He then wrote a facetious letter to the "publisher," that a "great person" had been half-starved by a "set of the most careless, blundering, foolish, crafty and knavish ministers that ever got in a house." The subtle references to ministers were deliberate. Franklin signed the article "Indignation."

In one small section of the *Gazette*, Franklin had a humorous stock report and death notice:

Stocks – Biscuits – very low

Buckwheat and Indian meal – both sour

Deaths – In the back closet and elsewhere, many poor mice

The Hutchinson Letters Scandal

In 1772, Benjamin Franklin obtained about ten letters written by Thomas Hutchinson, a Loyalist and the colonial governor of Massachusetts Bay Colony. The letters were written to several people in the ministry in England, primarily Thomas Whately, who was an advisor to England's prime minister. In the letters, Hutchinson grossly exaggerated the hostility of the colonists and included suggestions by his secretary, Andrew Oliver, that the Massachusetts colonists be more vigorously regulated by England. The purpose of these letters was to inflame tensions between England and the colonies. Franklin wisely realized that these letters represented deliberate mischaracterizations and were sent to selected members of the Parliament intended to bias them against the colonies. In one letter, Hutchinson said:

> There must be an abridgement of what are called English liberties...I doubt whether it is possible to project a system of government in which a colony, 3,000 miles distant from the parent state, shall enjoy all the liberty of the parent state...There must be a great restraint of natural liberty.

Franklin became alarmed by that and knew that the deeply incendiary nature of these letters could trigger a violent reaction on the part of Great Britain. Nevertheless, he felt it his duty to inform the colonial authorities of the treasonous nature of the writer's words but advised that the contents of these packets be kept private. He then sent the letters to the head of the colonial assembly in Massachusetts, Thomas Cushing.

Although the Hutchinson letters came to the attention of Samuel Adams of Boston, he kept them private but orchestrated a propaganda war against Hutchinson and Oliver. At that time, Samuel Adams was a member of the radical but clandestine Committees of Correspondence which held chapters in Massachusetts, Connecticut, New Hampshire, Rhode Island, and South Carolina, and which called for more forceful but non-violent resistance to English domination.

What made matters worse was the fact that portions of these letters were leaked to the press and published in the *Boston Gazette*. The colonists were furious. Effigies of Hutchinson and Oliver were burned in the streets of Boston and there were many demonstrations there. As knowledge of this betrayal by the colonial representatives spread around Boston, other uprisings occurred.

The Boston Tea Party and The Siege of Boston Harbor

In 1773, colonists, disguised as Native Americans, dumped over three hundred chests of tea leaves off a British vessel in Boston Harbor. This event stunned the seamen on the ship, most of whom had never seen a Native American before. Benjamin Franklin still had the mindset that he could placate the British and persuade them to see the relationship between the hostilities of the colonists and the excessive taxes that the king and Parliament were charging. In an attempt to appeal to their common sense and intelligence, he contacted Parliament with regard to the incident. First, he said that compensation would be made for the destruction of the tea, but balanced that comment with further qualifications. To reiterate what he had been telling them, Franklin issued a publication called "Hints for Conversation upon the Subject of Terms that might probably produce a Durable Union between Great Britain and the Colonies," in which he indicated that the tea tax and other taxes levied on trade with the colonies should all be repealed. After that, the colonies could reenact them if they wished, but the tax money should go into colonial treasuries, and its distribution should be controlled by colonial authorities, not British officials. Furthermore, Franklin stated that Parliament should have no control over the internal affairs of the colonies and should place no restrictions on the manufacture of goods in the colonies.

Following that, England blockaded the port of Boston. Instead of the regular English regimental units, the English hired Hessian mercenaries to execute the blockade. When William Pitt found out about that, he realized the injustice, not only because of the blockade but also the use of foreign mercenaries to do it. He was incensed at the behavior of the king and the Tories, saying, "If I were an American, as I am an Englishman, while a foreign troop was landed in my country, I would never lay down my arms—never! *Never!*

NEVER!" Franklin and his friend, William Pitt, then discussed the matter of the Boston Tea Party and the groundswell of animosity growing in the colonies. Pitt said that the colonies did, indeed, have the right to defend their rights, and he himself was making a strenuous effort in Parliament to alter the British stance on the dilemma. Franklin then delineated the grounds for colonial complaints and told Pitt that the injustices might even lead to open resistance; he basically predicted the Revolutionary War.

William Pitt asked Franklin to accompany him to a meeting of the House of Commons in the British Parliament. He and William Pitt approached the doorkeepers of the House, who graciously admitted them. Franklin, undergoing an attack of gout, limped in alongside Pitt. Pitt introduced a motion that the English vessels be withdrawn from Boston. There was a heated debate following that, but the majority of the members in the House voted against it. Pitt then worked on a draft of a compromise plan and conferred with Franklin about it. Franklin noted that there were so many caveats in the proposal that he rejected it. Pitt then redrafted it and returned. This plan would, in effect, represent an agreement between Britain and the colonies that—it was hoped—would bring about a reconciliation between the two parties. This time, Franklin approved it, and Pitt brought him back into the House where it would be analyzed. Franklin and Pitt had support from some of the members. However, Edward Montagu rose up and became belligerent. He loudly accused Franklin of writing the proposal himself, saying the American had written it and he was a "bitter and mischievous enemy." Pitt calmly assured the assembly that he himself had written the proposal. The House retorted that it was "weak" and "bad." Montagu and Pitt argued vehemently, and the whole assembly joined in. Everyone in the room was shouting. In the end, the House of Commons laid the proposal aside and tabled the motion. Pitt sensed that this whole episode would have explosive consequences and warned everyone against harassing the colonists. He also approached the monarch about it, but King George ignored him.

Franklin was astounded. In his memoirs, he wrote:

> To hear so many of the hereditary legislators declaiming so
> vehemently against, not adopting merely, but even
> the consideration of a proposal so important in its nature,
> offered by a person of so weighty a character ... gave me an
> exceeding mean opinion of their abilities, and made their
> claim of sovereignty over three millions of virtuous sensible
> people in America, seem the greatest of absurdities, since
> they appeared to have scarce discretion enough to govern a
> herd of swine.

Appearance Before the Privy Council in England

Benjamin Franklin was called before the Privy Council around
March of 1774, once they were informed about the Hutchinson
letters. Franklin's friend, Dr. Priestley, through the intercession of
Edmund Burke, gained admission to the meeting.

In the initial introductory session, the speaker of the Council,
Solicitor General Alexander Wedderburn, defended England's
approval of Hutchinson as colonial governor by pointing out his
virtues:

> His Majesty's choice followed the wishes of his people; and
> no other man could have been named whom so many
> favorable circumstances concurred to recommend. A native
> the country (of America), whose ancestors were among its
> first settlers.

Wedderburn characterized the affair as being a misunderstanding
and that the collection consisted of private letters "stolen by Dr.
Franklin," whose motive was to become governor of Massachusetts.
Then they intimated that Franklin himself contrived against the
governor and Oliver. Next, the Council spent its follow-up
interrogation trying to ferret out the identity of the person who gave
Franklin the letters. Throughout the entire proceedings, Franklin

never revealed the name of the person who gave him those letters. To this day, no one knows who that person was.

At the close of the meeting, Wedderburn upheld the innocence of Hutchinson and Oliver and went on a tireless harangue against the character of Franklin. An observer at the meeting said that Benjamin Franklin stood like a rock "abiding the pelting of a pitiless storm." The Privy Council admitted that there were no grounds to bring any charges against Dr. Franklin but did see to it that he was dismissed from his position as postmaster general of the colonies. Fortunately, his son-in-law, Richard Bache, had been working under him as secretary and comptroller and took over the position.

Word about these disdainful proceedings circulated in the colonies. The colonists felt immediate sympathy for Franklin and admired him for the courage it took to face the Privy Council itself and emerge unscathed. He was now 68 years old and had stood for nearly three hours in the Council's chambers because no one offered him a chair. The citizens of Philadelphia burned both Hutchinson and Wedderburn in effigy. After that, Hutchinson moved to England and faded into history. Wedderburn initially was celebrated, but later historians dismissed him as being superficial and even vulgar.

After spending nearly seventeen years representing the colonies in England, Franklin realized he must leave. He had done all he could to prevent the relationship between America and England from accelerating into war. After hearing the attitudes of King George III and his supporters, he became wholly committed to the cause for freedom.

In 1774, the colonists held their second meeting of the Continental Congress. Fifty-one of the colonial delegates to this Congress signed a petition addressed to King George III of Britain, listing a number of their grievances. In the petition, they asked the king directly to exert all efforts to address these issues. They sent a copy of it to Franklin along with an attached cover letter to him from Charles Thomson, the secretary of the Congress. It was signed by John

Dickinson, who wrote the final draft, and John Hancock, Roger Sherman, Charles Thomson, John Adams, John Jay, and Thomas Jefferson. Franklin read it and added his signature to it. This document became known as the Olive Branch Petition. The king himself, however, had already declared that the colonies were in open rebellion, and refused to read it!

Unfortunately, Franklin found himself firmly opposing those Englishmen who were once his supporters and friends. Franklin's friend, William Strahan, developed a more hostile attitude toward Franklin and the patriotic cause. Now disillusioned with Strahan's sudden lack of empathy for the American position, Franklin wrote to Strahan in 1775 saying that he, as a member of Parliament, was one of the majority who doomed America to destruction. Franklin said, "You have begun to burn our towns and murder our people...You and I were long friends; you are now my enemy, and I am yours."

Welcome Worn Out

The Massachusetts patriot, Samuel Adams, had the impression that Franklin wasn't really committed to the principles of liberty that the colonies were promoting. That wasn't true. While in England, Franklin spoke up to justify reasons for the behavior of the colonists who were reacting, sometimes violently, to the domination of England. Nevertheless, in America, Franklin was considered "too English," and in England, he was considered "too American." The atmosphere was getting much too controversial in England. Franklin knew that he had done his utmost to mend the breach between Great Britain and the colonies, but no longer felt he could do anything more there. Franklin also desperately wanted to return home.

His children were so much older now. His daughter, Sally, had married and had two children of her own. He dearly missed his wife and felt guilty for having left her for so long—eleven years altogether. They did correspond, and he often sent her gifts. In 1772, he was concerned because she had some health concerns and gave her some advice in terms of certain foods to avoid. Historians have presented two theories about why Deborah didn't accompany him to England. One is that she was afraid of traveling across the ocean, and the other one, taken from her own words, indicates that she feared she wouldn't look that presentable to the fashionable English ladies and would embarrass Benjamin.

As he was preparing to leave for America, Franklin received word that she died. Friends said that he was extremely upset about the loss, which he hadn't anticipated. There was no prolonged illness on her part, and it was later reported that she died suddenly of a massive stroke.

In December 1774, Franklin left Great Britain. While he was at sea, the American Revolution broke out. It was triggered by the Battles of Lexington and Concord in 1775. Franklin wrote to Edmund Burke about the event and described the frenzied retreat of the English commander, General Gage: "General Gage's troops made a most vigorous retreat—twenty miles in three hours!—scarcely to be paralleled in history."

Bones in the Basement

While living on Craven Street in London, Ben Franklin took in a lodger by the name of William Hewson who was a surgeon. In his lodging in the basement, he taught anatomy and held laboratory classes. The practice of grave-robbing and human dissection was deemed criminal in the 18th century. Because medical students sorely needed to learn firsthand about anatomy, the practice continued but was performed under the cover of darkness. Men would creep around the graveyards disinterring corpses or snatching bodies from the gallows. Then they squirreled them away to sell to clandestine labs like Hewson's. In 1998, when the residence was being restored for museum purposes, the skeletons of four adults and six children were discovered buried under Franklin's house. Colin Schultze reported in the *Smithsonian*: "From a one-metre-wide, one-metre-deep pit, over 1200 pieces of bone were retrieved." The historians of the Ben Franklin House there, which eventually became a museum, indicated that Franklin most likely knew that this activity was being conducted.

Chapter 8 – Home and on to France

Franklin was home briefly and stayed with his grown daughter, Sarah, whom he called "Sally," and her husband, Richard Bache, along with their child, Benjamin. However, Benjamin startled them one day by bringing with him William Tempe Franklin, the illegitimate son of his eldest son.

Ben was pleased to discover that Sally was contributing to the Revolutionary War efforts by sewing uniforms for the troops. Not only that, but she motivated a number of Quaker women in Pennsylvania to help. Quakers, by virtue of their religious beliefs, weren't permitted to enlist in the military, but a family friend said that Sarah showed great persuasiveness and "… courage in asking, which surpassed even the obstinate reluctance of the Quakers in refusing."

Richard Bache had a grocery store and also served on the Pennsylvania Board of War. He also functioned as the head of the new political group, the Republican Society in Pennsylvania.

Franklin's Break with His Son

With great disappointment, Franklin discovered that his son, William, who had accompanied him to England, was a committed Loyalist. With Franklin's help, William was installed as governor of New Jersey, but William spent his time vigorously working against American interests for freedom. In 1776, William was arrested by the Provincial Congress of New Jersey for treasonous behavior and placed under the custody of an American merchant. However, while there, William continued to send information about American troops to the British. Once that was discovered in 1777, Pennsylvania transferred him to a dismal jail in Litchfield, Connecticut. When the sheriff, Lynde Lord, arrived to oversee the jail, he then moved the young man into solitary confinement. The cell had no furniture or toilet facilities. Reportedly, Ben Franklin didn't intervene to help. While William was there, his wife died.

Next, Governor Trumbull of Connecticut transferred him to East Windsor, Connecticut. He became ill while there. After a long period in recovery, a prisoner exchange was arranged, and he was released. Soon afterward, William emigrated to England where he spent the remainder of his life. When Ben Franklin was much older, he wrote to William expressing his extreme disappointment saying, "Nothing has ever hurt me so much and affected me with such keen sensations as to find myself deserted in my old age by my only son, and not only deserted, but to find him taking up arms against me, in a cause wherein my good fame, fortune and life were all at stake." Franklin had now lost his wife and his son, too, in a sense. When he rewrote his will, Benjamin left nothing to William.

The Declaration of Independence

In 1775, Dr. Franklin was elected as a delegate to the Second Continental Congress. Franklin, now 69 years old, did attend a few of the initial sessions for the drafting of the Declaration of Independence. However, he was ill during much of that time with gout and didn't attend too many of the early sessions. When he returned in better health, Franklin, Thomas Jefferson, Robert Livingston, John Adams, and Robert Sherman were selected to help draft the document. Jefferson was an eloquent young statesman and writer, and he wrote the Declaration, asking Franklin to advise him at times. Benjamin Franklin signed it, along with the other delegates, but it needed to be ratified by all of the colonies. With the Declaration of Independence, the colonies would then be enabled to attempt to get military and logistical support from other countries because the document was a definitive declaration of war.

Pennsylvania Constitution

In 1776, immediately after the Continental Congress, Franklin was elected to the presidency of the Pennsylvania Assembly that was tasked with drawing up its own constitution. The colonial charter set up while England controlled America was abrogated. During the discussions about the new Pennsylvanian constitution, Franklin especially campaigned for its declaration of rights. This was a plainly worded but forceful statement that "all men have a natural right to worship Almighty God according to the dictates of their own consciences and understanding, and that no man ought to or be compelled to attend any religious worship." Franklin was very firm on that issue throughout life.

America's Ambassador to France

In October of 1776, Ben Franklin was appointed ambassador to France and was sent there on a confidential mission to secure their support for the American Revolution. America had no navy and lacked sufficient military equipment. Franklin left immediately and took his two grandsons, William Temple Franklin and Benjamin Franklin Bache. During their trip across the Atlantic, they underwent a number of frightening storms and were even attacked by English vessels on the way.

Maintaining the secrecy of the trip proved to be impossible. Franklin's experiments with electricity and his invention of the lightning rod had already reached France and stunned the French community. Already the invention of the Armonica was known there, and the French queen had entertained her friends with the instrument at their dinners.

One of the reasons Franklin hoped to maintain secrecy was the fact that the French foreign minister, Comte de Vergennes, had been smuggling French-made weapons to America in violation of the export ban in place at the time. In 1779, Franklin had also secretly obtained funds from France to have some ships built to be used for privateering. Captain Paul Jones was in command of that fleet and called his flagship the *Bonhomme Richard*, meaning a "sugar baby," which was a play on the words *Poor Richard's Almanac*. Furthermore, France didn't want to trigger a conflict between themselves and England if they found out about Benjamin Franklin's visit prior to any potential agreement.

Unfortunately, the merchant Silas Deane, who was involved with the secret shipment of arms to the colonies, wasted no time at all in telling other colleagues that Franklin was in France, and gossip raced all over Paris. Although Franklin sneaked down the Seine in a simple rowboat, he was met with crowds of well-wishers, and a welcome dinner was held for him in Nantes.

After the affair, he was brought by coach to his hotel. Again, he was greeted by cheering crowds along the streets. Shortly thereafter, Count Jacques-Donatien de Chaumont invited Franklin and his grandsons to stay at his chateau instead. De Chaumont was a noble who was a firm supporter of the American Revolution and often aided support to the American colonies.

After his arrival at the Chateau de Chaumont, Franklin sent his youngest grandchild to a French school, Le Coeur's, that taught English-speaking students from the colonies. As for his 15-year-old grandchild, William, Franklin sent him to Geneva where he could gain experience in a foreign country.

Franklin was a charismatic and ingenious character. His remarkable uniqueness made him a curiosity, and the French people admired him for his individuality. Instead of the traditional powdered wig and elaborate coiffure typical of political leaders, Franklin wore a fur cap and dressed plainly. The French were intrigued by him. In fact, he became so popular there that his likeness appeared on snuffboxes, medallions, watches, and rings!

After reporting to his office at the Chateau, Franklin found out that Prime Minister North discovered he was in France. North made a desperate attempt to stop the Revolutionary War. No more were there any delays in communications. North contacted Franklin promising that England would stop taxing the colonists altogether, adding that the Americans would no longer be considered "rebels," but "His Majesty's faithful subjects." Franklin didn't respond. Revolutions cannot suddenly reverse themselves.

The nobleman and military strategist, the Marquis de Lafayette, was already committed to the American cause before there was any alliance established between America and France. Without securing official permission, Lafayette sailed for America having financed his own voyage. He accompanied George Washington early in the war. When Lafayette returned to France, he met the eloquent Ben Franklin. Together they worked to secure full French support.

In 1777, the colonists prevailed over General Burgoyne at the battlefields in Saratoga, New York. This was a decisive victory and was the turning point in the American Revolution. General Burgoyne was considered by both the English and the French as one of the most capable military commanders of England, and the Saratoga victory demonstrated the depth of the American commitment to the cause of freedom. The French court took notice of this success, giving them the confidence they needed to enter the war as America's ally.

In the meantime, the British ambassador to France, Lord Stormont, spread false rumors throughout France that the initial battles of the American Revolution were resulting in loss after loss. When visitors asked Franklin about whether or not that was true, Franklin replied, "Oh no, it is not the truth. It is only a *Stormont*." The term "Stormont" became a synonym for lying, and the French people loved to laugh at it.

The drafts of two treaties were drawn up by Franklin, Silas Deane, and Arthur Lee, an agent sent along later from the colonies. The first was the Treaty of Alliance, by which each party agreed to defend the other if either was attacked by the British. An offer was also extended to other interested nations to join with America in its fight for independence; Spain and the Dutch Republic responded that they were indeed interested in assisting the cause. The second draft was the Treaty of Amity and Commerce. By virtue of the amity treaty, France recognized America as an independent nation and was granted certain exclusive shipping and trading rights. Franklin then obtained a copy of the constitution of each colony. After gathering all these documents, Franklin sent a message to the court at Versailles, asking to see King Louis XVI. The king responded, saying the parties could meet at the Hotel de Crillon in Paris.

In 1778, the treaties were signed. France made the Comte de Rochambeau the commander of an expeditionary force, and he proceeded requisitioning men, equipment, and supplies. With him, he brought Lafayette and several ships containing over 6,000 French soldiers, supplies, and armaments. Lafayette excitedly contacted George Washington, saying,

There is nothing to be found in France which might offer to me so delightful a prospect as those ships and troops. Everything will be soon provided for and we shall be able within these few days to set off at a moment's warning so that our expeditions will go very well.

A famous English author and historian, Edward Gibbon, often visited France and dined at the French cafes there. Franklin's time-tested technique consisted of contacting well-known men and establishing relationships with them. One time, when Franklin spotted him at a cafe, he slipped Gibbon a note inviting him for a drink. It was intended as a simple gesture of cordiality and a matter of intellectual curiosity. Gibbon sent him back a note with a haughty response saying that he wouldn't speak to a "rebel." Franklin sarcastically responded in a follow-up note suggesting that Gibbon's next book should be the "Decline and Fall of the British Empire!" a play on Gibbon's famous book *The Decline and Fall of the Roman Empire*.

The Troublesome John Adams

The Continental Congress appointed the well-known patriot, John Adams, as a commissioner to France. He arrived in France several months after the Treaty of Alliance and the Treaty of Amity and Commerce were signed. Adams met with Franklin and Lee but disapproved of both of them. In addition, he harbored a distrust of France. Adams felt France had a greedy self-interest in the trade and commerce treaty. Lee, Franklin, and Adams had a number of arguments about it as a result of Adams' pessimism. Adams then drafted a letter to the Comte de Vergennes, demanding more naval vessels. After Franklin read it, he toned down the emotional language and sent it on. De Vergennes responded indicating that their fleet was also engaged in the West Indies, one of their territories. He also communicated with Adams and the Continental Congress regarding their full commitment to support the cause of America's freedom. In America, the French Navy later sent Admiral de Barras north from the West Indies to America to rendezvous with George Washington, Lafayette, and Rochambeau in Virginia. It is unknown as to whether or not Adams was instrumental in bringing that about, or if it was Lafayette's intervention.

In 1780, the Continental dollar was devalued, and Adams was summoned to see de Vergennes. The French were concerned that this currency downturn would upset trade relations with France if America won the war. De Vergennes asked Adams to make an exception for the French merchants. Adams adamantly refused and defended the congressional decision regarding the currency. However, he didn't stop there. He followed up with a diatribe listing his other grievances about France and objected to any exclusive trading rights with France. This alarmed de Vergennes, who felt that any subsequent American trade agreement with England would threaten France. Historically, John Adams was a very outspoken man, who often spoke before he considered what another's response might be. Many of his written contributions to the Continental Congress were strongly worded, and fellow members frequently had to soften the wording in those documents.

In fact, de Vergennes himself personally disliked Adams and even wrote to the Continental Congress stating that he would only deal with Franklin and requested that the Congress appoint Benjamin Franklin as the sole plenipotentiary minister to France. Congress did so, and Adams was transferred to the Dutch Republic to talk about its interest in supporting America. The Continental Congress transferred Arthur Lee to Spain because that country was also interested in joining the war effort.

The Troubles Continue

Adams' foreign policy was influenced by a pamphlet by Thomas Pownall, the former lieutenant-governor of New Jersey. In it, Pownall indicated that it was essential that the Revolutionary War be concluded as soon as possible so that Great Britain and America could reestablish trade with each other. The war wasn't yet over, but

Adams impatiently made incessant efforts to have England draw up a peace treaty with America. In 1780, Adams wrote a letter saying that America should also be allowed to conduct trade with Great Britain, saying "...no other nation would be able to rival England in those manufactures which we most want in America."

There were a number of letters exchanged between Adams and some of the colonists having to do with Adams' concerns about the trade agreement. After that, Adams published his letter, along with other related ones. Fortunately, they weren't printed until 1782 just before the war ended. Had the French read Adams' publication earlier, it is quite possible that they would have pulled out of the treaties of alliance.

In the year 1781, the theater of operations in the American Revolution switched from the Northern to the Southern colonies. General de Rochambeau, who had been dispatched from France, was instrumental in working with George Washington as the commander-in-chief. Rochambeau and Washington focused their attention on the English threat in Yorktown and fought to expel the British. Due to the overwhelming support that came from the French Navy, Washington and the French allies ended the American Revolution in victory.

When Prime Minister North got word of the momentous victory of America at Yorktown and the surrender of their lieutenant-general, Charles Cornwallis, he shouted, "O God! It is all over!"

Benjamin Franklin: A Faux Pas

In 1782, Comte de Vergennes, the foreign minister of France, proposed the culminating treaty between England and America. Together they drew up a document called the Peace of Paris, which determined the borders of America and granted fishing rights off of Newfoundland to France. Great Britain made concessions to France by granting it control of the islands of Tobago and Senegal, two tropical colonies that France always craved possession of. Franklin then secured the agreement of the Comte de Vergennes for the Peace of Paris. De Vergennes was delighted that he could be included in the settlement, signed it, and moved the process along rapidly through the legal process. This treaty wasn't destined to go into effect until it was signed by both the Americans and Great Britain, however.

Back home, America didn't approve of the Peace of Paris. For one thing, America wanted to cut Comte de Vergennes out of the negotiations. To resolve what they saw as weaknesses in the Franklin-Vergennes peace treaty, they sent John Adams back to France, along with John Jay and Henry Laurens, to work with Franklin on drawing up a revised treaty. America also felt that separate negotiations should be set up with England as well as Spain. To accomplish that, John Jay traveled to England and contacted its prime minister, Lord Shelburne. The existence of two possible treaties was a political embarrassment, especially in view of the fact that the Comte de Vergennes wasn't going to be included in the final settlement, which left Franklin in an awkward situation. Franklin was then ordered to offer an apology to de Vergennes for the confusion.

The Treaty of Paris

Problems often happen when treaties are negotiated, especially when various diplomats compete in order to receive the credit for negotiating. John Jay and Shelburne set up a treaty more favorable to England than to France in terms of trading rights, but it acknowledged American independence. This treaty granted America the right to occupy all of the land east of the Mississippi River up to the southern border of Canada. America would have the right to fish off the waters of Canada. In addition, any property confiscated from legal British owners would be returned to them.

Spain received Florida, with the exception of some smaller territories north and northwest of there, and Menorca. Grenada and Montserrat in the West Indies had been conquered by the Spanish and French but were returned to England as a result of the treaty.

France was granted rights to Tobago and Senegal, which is something de Vergennes had wanted when he and Franklin had worked out the defunct Peace of Paris. France also was given the right to fish off the coast of Newfoundland.

In 1783, the Treaty of Paris was signed by David Hartley and Richard Oswald representing King George III of England, and Franklin, Jay, Laurens, and Adams on behalf of America.

After the signing of the Treaty of Paris, a story circulated around Paris about a dinner that was held with the English ambassador, David Hartley, Richard Oswald, the French king's minister, and Ben Franklin. Hartley offered a toast to the king whom he said was like the sun at midday. Oswald drank to the health of King Louis XVI of France. Franklin lifted his glass very high and toasted George Washington, adding that the commander-in-chief was like Joshua in the Bible who made the sun and moon stand still, and "…they obeyed him!"

When Thomas Jefferson was sent to France as the next ambassador in 1784, the Comte de Vergennes asked him if he was going to replace Franklin. Jefferson, who admired Franklin immensely, replied, "No one can replace him, sir; I am only his successor."

Relationship with John Adams

John Adams was always annoyed by Franklin's casual manner and off-handed remarks, and never fully trusted him. When Franklin made the mistake of introducing Adams to one of his French female friends, he was scandalized by the woman's seductive appearance. Abigail Adams, John Adams' wife, was horrified when the Frenchwoman kissed Franklin, although she merely kissed him on the cheek. In a couple of her letters to friends, Abigail said that the woman threw her arms around Franklin, and appeared rather unkempt and slovenly in appearance—thoroughly lacking in manners. She and her husband had been raised in a strict Puritan household, where they were taught that people should be very restrained and proper. In addition, Adams—who was much more formal in his communication with foreign dignitaries—was taken aback by Franklin's use of French vocabulary. Franklin had taught himself French, but Adams was educated in the use of the language. In addition, there are pronunciations of French which are considered more proper and is referred to as the "Parisian dialect." According to French contemporaries, Franklin's use of French was considered adequate, although he made grammatical errors. Even though Adams was formerly educated in French and thought he spoke it fluently, the French people themselves criticized him, saying that he often had to search for words.

The enmity of Lee, Adams, and Jay for Franklin grew, but Franklin adroitly avoided any outward show of hostility. Thomas Jefferson, the rising statesman and Virginia delegate, expressed concern about the comportment of Adams as a negotiator at all. He is recorded to have said that Adams "hates John Jay, hates the French and hates the English."

The French respected Franklin more than they did Adams, and Adams appeared to be jealous of Franklin's ability as a diplomat, although he did recognize it. Adams once said about Franklin that he "...is always an honest man, often a wise one, but sometimes in some things, absolutely out of his senses." It is unfortunate that personal feelings interfered with foreign relations.

Franklin's "Women"

Even though he was 70 years old, Franklin was what is called a "ladies' man." His wit and charm attracted a number of women, and he didn't resist their charms either. Upper-class women used to crowd around him and engage in light-hearted conversations and jokes.

Elisabeth, Countess d'Houdetot, and her husband had what one might call an "open relationship," and the countess often had affairs with other men. When Franklin was in France, he was entertained at her house. Reportedly, she wasn't very good-looking but was a quick wit. That drew Franklin to her, and they exchanged sarcastic and amusing barbs.

Another woman that Franklin met was Madame Helvetius, the widow of Claude Helvetius, a philosopher. She once was offended that Franklin didn't ask to spend a night together with her. To that, he replied, "Madame, I am waiting until the nights are longer." Franklin visited her often, as he enjoyed her sense of humor and her intelligence as well as her affection. It was said that Franklin did actually propose to her and bemoaned the fact that she wouldn't marry him. Franklin even wrote a somewhat suggestive letter to her couched within a facetious analogy which he told about a fictitious dream in which Socrates spoke to him about Helvetius. In the story, Socrates said, "I will confess to you that I loved her extremely, but she was cruel to me, and rejected me."

Franklin's mind then wandered to thoughts about his deceased wife and continued his stream of consciousness:

> ...Then I saw Mrs. Franklin. I reclaimed her, but she answered me coldly and said "I have been a good wife to you for forty-nine years and four months, nearly half a century; let that content you. I have formed a new connection here which will last to eternity."

Perhaps that sprang from guilt because Franklin was away from her for so long.

Although it was a platonic relationship, he and Madame Brillon de Jouy, who was married, often associated with each other. She called Ben Franklin "*Mon Cher Papa*," that is, "My Dear Papa." Once when he passed her house while Mme. Brillon was away for a prolonged period, Franklin wrote to her saying,

> I often pass your house; it appears desolate now to me...I find the Commandments very inconvenient and I am sorry they were made. If, in your travels, you happen to see the Holy Father, you might ask him to repeal them, as having

been given only to Jews and too hard for good Christians to keep.

It was said that she responded to Franklin, saying she absolved him of all sin, "present, past and future." Franklin even shared stories about his relationship with Madame Helvetius with Madame Brillon. She then quipped, "Give this evening to my amiable rival, Madame Helvetius, kiss her for yourself and for another…and I grant you the power of attorney to visit my neighbor, Mademoiselle Le Veillard."

Franklin actually did try to visit Mademoiselle Le Veillard, but she wasn't in when he arrived. When she heard about this visit, the mademoiselle went to Franklin's house who funnily enough wasn't in at the time. She then left a note on Franklin's door saying, "Mademoiselle Le Veillard came by to have the honor to be kissed by Monsieur Franklin."

Madame Brillon's husband—dismayed by Franklin's frequent appearances—wanted to keep Franklin from seeing his wife in case the liaison escalated. So, he introduced Franklin to Madame Foucault, saying, "She is marvelously plump once again and has just acquired new curves. Very round curves, very white, they seem to have a quality most essential in the eyes of amateurs such as you. It would be possible, I bet, to kill a flea on them."

King Louis XVI knew of Franklin's attraction to women, and theirs for him. He then saw it for himself at a celebration in his court. The women fawned all over him to the point that the king considered it quite inappropriate. He then had a chamber pot designed and sent to a high-ranking French countess, Diane de Polignac. The chamber pot had Franklin's likeness in the bottom of it!

Franklin didn't shy away from his experience and knowledge of women, and once wrote a letter entitled, "Advice to a Young Man on the Choice of a Mistress." In it, he advised the man to select an older woman because there would be no danger in having children, and she would most likely be discreet about an affair, an affair which would prevent a man from "…ruining his health and fortune among mercenary prostitutes." Curiously enough, however, publication of that letter wasn't released until the 19th century and has been used as a rationale for repealing obscenity laws.

His Farewell to France

Dr. Franklin was now 79 years old and rather infirm. Joseph Bentham, a printer for the University of Cambridge, was a witness during Franklin's appearance before the Privy Council in England. He said that Dr. Franklin was very debilitated by some respiratory ailments and said that, "...even his voice was so husky and choked with phlegm, that it refused utterance to the sentiments which were directed by his superior intelligence." Franklin's respiratory condition grew worse with time, and he was occasionally bedridden while in France.

When he was preparing to leave France, Franklin wanted to personally bid farewell to the Comte de Vergennes but was prevented from doing so because of his increasing debility. Instead, he sent a letter to him saying:

> May I beg the favor of you, Sir, to express respectfully for me to His Majesty, the deep sense I have for all the inestimable benefits his goodness has conferred on my country; a sentiment that it will be the business of the little remainder of the life now left to me, to impress equally on the minds of all my countrymen.

Accompanying a letter of gratitude, the king sent Franklin a portrait of himself embedded with jewels, mostly diamonds. It is still very valuable and is located in the Smithsonian National Portrait Gallery in Washington, D.C.

Chapter 9 – Benjamin Franklin's Last Years

In 1785, Franklin returned home. The people of Philadelphia crowded the wharf on Market Street to greet him. A great cannon was fired and bells rang from all the churches. His son-in-law, Richard, was there with the throngs of people who cheered and followed his coach as he went home to see the rest of his family.

His status as a statesman and Founding Father was appreciated, and he was called upon in 1787 to serve in the Pennsylvania Assembly once again. He was also unanimously elected as president of the Supreme Executive Council of Pennsylvania and served in that capacity until 1788. The prestige and weight of that appointment was as important as the position of governor. The Supreme Council formulated the constitution of the Commonwealth of Pennsylvania. Franklin contributed to that formulation, and the finalized constitution was passed in 1790. He served for three years, but was becoming more ill and had to retire.

Later in 1787, Franklin was called upon to participate in the Constitutional Convention. Because he was in his 80s and very frail, he didn't speak often during those sessions. Occasionally, he had another Pennsylvanian delegate, James Wilson, read some of his contributions aloud for the assembly.

The Constitutional Convention

When he attended the Constitutional Convention, Franklin was seated next to George Washington, who sat in a chair with the picture of a sun on the back of it. The Convention argued about boundary lines, and the colonies broke out in arguments over trade and the payment of war debt. Washington became frustrated that his new nation already seemed to be breaking into fragments. He stood up and boldly and said to the assembly, "We are one nation today. Will we be thirteen tomorrow?"

The members of the Convention wrestled with its wording, and the process dragged on for a month. Franklin didn't entirely approve of the final draft of the Constitution, due to his concerns with some of the issues about trade, slavery, taxes, and foreign affairs. He felt, and history bore him out, that those factors would cause contention in the future. However, he saw a great deal of quality within the new Constitution, saying that it was near perfection. He also felt that members of the Convention should approve of it in its current form, but remain open to making some changes in the future due to changing circumstances. He said, "I doubt whether any other convention we can obtain may be able to make a better Constitution." Some people wanted to put it off until Washington rushed forward and signed it. Once Washington signed, the others signed in quick succession.

After the signatories signed the Constitution, Franklin glanced at the sun painted on the back of Washington's chair and said:

> I have often and often in the course of the session…looked at the sun behind the president (George Washington, president of the assembly), without being able to tell whether or not it

was rising or setting. But now, at length, I have the happiness to know that it is a rising and not a setting sun.

Franklin and Paper Currency

During the sessions of the Constitutional Convention, the issue of the payment of war debt also arose. This reawakened Franklin's earlier views on the advantages of using paper money, rather than relying on gold and silver to pay debts.

Franklin wrote essays fostering the use of paper currency in 1740 and defended its usage. Gold and silver could only be procured through foreign trade for the most part, and that had created difficulties in the past. If there were shortages of these metals, it would stifle trade, even that between the colonies. Needless to say, carrying sacks of coins in order to purchase items was clumsy and cumbersome. In his treatise, "A Modest Enquiry into the Nature and Necessity of Paper Money," he said, "Money as a currency has additional value by so much time and labor as it saves in the exchange of commodities." He also pointed out the fact that, if there was a scarcity of gold and silver, people might have to resort to bartering in order to purchase goods. Wisely, he pointed out that the precious metals tend to vary in value.

He further cautioned that the amount of paper currency issued must be limited by assets that could be designated to maintain its assessed valuation, or inflation would occur. As a backup asset, Franklin proposed land. Later on, he altered that notion by indicating that silver be used instead of land as security.

Banks, he said, would be well situated to stabilize quantities of currency in circulation. Today, economists use the term "money in circulation," or "M1." Franklin indicated that a well-run bank would never loan more money than its landed securities allowed for. In recent years, that principle he advocated has been violated, causing bank failures and the depreciation of a country's currency in the global market. Actually, that happened in America following the

American Revolution when banks paid for war debts in the hopes that they could later charge taxes to cover the costs.

During the American Revolution, Continental currency was counterfeited by the British and its usage was suspended. That caused some disastrous results when George Washington's troops refused to continue in their march through New Jersey because the currency that was used for their wages was valueless. He was then forced to borrow gold and silver from one of his allies during the war. A standardized system was needed that was less vulnerable to counterfeiting and fully secured by collateral in the banks. This would build confidence and help with getting the currency accepted by all parties.

Franklin had plans to wrestle with the problem of counterfeiting, which he indicated could be resolved in the printing process. When he had a contract to print money for New Jersey in 1730, it was said that it didn't easily lend itself to counterfeiting.

It is unknown as to how he weighed in on the issue of paper currency at the Constitutional Convention. However, in view of Franklin's general attitude toward the use of paper currency, it would be safe to conclude that he was in favor of it, but with the caveat that the monetary system be handled responsibly.

Benjamin Franklin and Slavery

When Benjamin Franklin was a young man, he held prejudicial views about Black people. In 1730, he compared "the sauciness of a Negro" to the "prattle of a child." He also wrote about African Americans in economic terms when he estimated the cost of losing slaves to smallpox. In the *Pennsylvania Gazette*, he continually published advertisements for slave owners who were trying to recover their runaway slaves. While he wasn't a slave trader, one could say that he was a broker—an intermediary between sellers and buyers of slaves, which led to a conclusion by some historians that he was a slave trader, even if in a limited sense.

For example, he advertised the sale of "A likely young Negro fellow, about twenty-six years of age, suitable for any farming or plantation business, having been long accustomed to it and has had the smallpox." And, "To be sold. A prime able young Negro man, fit for laborious work in town or country, that has had the smallpox. As also a middle-aged Negro man that has likewise had the smallpox. Inquire of the printer hereof, or otherwise they will be exposed to sale by public venue." When Franklin went to England, he brought his slave, Peter, with him. Later, he complained about Peter's behavior saying that he was "of little use and often in mischief," but he did add that they had a good relationship. Sometimes he spoke about Black people saying that they "misbehave," a term used when speaking of a disobedient child rather than an adult. He even put an advertisement in his *Pennsylvania Gazette* for Peter when he ran away. Yet, if he felt that Peter wasn't useful, why did he bother?

Like other colonists, he thought that Black people were inherently inferior to Caucasians. In his "Observations on the Increase of Mankind" published in 1755, there was a section on nonwhites, with the exception of the tribal people who were the first natives of America. In the essay, he asked, "Why increase the sons of Africa by planting them in America, where we have so fair an opportunity, by excluding all Black people and Tawneys, of increasing the lovely white and red?" However, he later remarked that he was "partial to the complexion of my country." Some elements of white supremacy do appear to be present.

Besides the ads about the sale of slaves, Franklin also printed letters from those who were promoting the cause of abolitionism in the colonies. In 1740, he informed the public that Reverend George Whitefield was seeking to build a "Negro school" in the colony, and included a solicitation for donations that could be sent to the "printer" of the newspaper for that purpose. Due to the fact that America was beginning to espouse equality for all men, Franklin realized that he had to reexamine his own beliefs.

In the early 1760s, Franklin met Thomas Bray, an Anglican minister in England, who contacted him in regards to sending out missionaries to convert Black people and building schools for them in the colonies. Franklin was enthusiastic and encouraged him to do so. In 1758, Bray set up a small school in Pennsylvania, which was successful. Prior to her death, Franklin's wife wrote to him in England praising the effort after she herself had attended some classes that Bray already had opened. During that year, Franklin visited some of the schools he had a hand in establishing and wrote,

> I have conceived a higher opinion of the natural capacities of the black race than I had ever before entertained. Their apprehension seems as quick, their memory as strong, and their docility in every respect equal to that of white children.

After that, Franklin started altering his opinion and wrote that these perceived negative characteristics he and others had stemmed not from race, but from poor education, negative environments, and the institution of slavery itself. In 1760, Franklin was appointed chairman of Bray's Associates. He also recommended that William Dawson, the president of the College of William and Mary, open a school in Virginia for Black people. According to his correspondence, Franklin became more active in promoting education for Black people in Rhode Island in 1763.

He joined the Pennsylvania Society Promoting the Abolition of Slavery and the Relief of Free Negroes Unlawfully Held in Bondage in the 1780s. When he was elected president of the society, he appended their charter and outlined procedures he deemed appropriate before anyone freed their slaves. This Franklin called the "Plan for Improving the Condition of the Free Blacks, 1789." Then he set up 24 subcommittees to the task of providing apprenticeships for them. It should be noted that the thesis Franklin wrote was about only those who were free Black people.

He also supported the Quaker abolitionist, Anthony Benezet, in his founding of a school for Black people in Philadelphia. In 1758, Franklin opened several free schools for Black people and financially gave them support.

In 1787, he was elected the president of the Abolitionist Society, and published letters to the public on behalf of the group and sent a petition to Congress to promote the cause of abolishing slavery altogether. One of the questionable issues that he cited at the Constitutional Convention had to do with slavery. Insightfully, he realized that simply freeing slaves would be a disservice if it wasn't accompanied with providing them with skills related to education and the tools they would need to secure gainful employment, as well as some financial support to start out.

Just three months before his death in 1790, Franklin sent an official petition to Congress which stated:

> From a persuasion that equal liberty was originally the portion, it is still the birthright of all men, and influenced by the strong ties of humanity and the principles of their institution, your memorialists conceive themselves bound to use all justifiable endeavors to loosen the bounds of slavery and promote a general enjoyment of the blessings of freedom.

There are no consistent records as to what actually happened to Franklin's slaves in the 1780s. He did have a clause in his 1757 will for the freeing of his two slaves upon death. While Franklin supported the abolition movement and education of Black people, he wasn't ever outspoken about it. His stance on the issue would seem to be ambiguous.

Contrary View

In his book, *Runaway America: Benjamin Franklin, Slavery, and the American Revolution*, Dr. Waldstreicher of Temple University indicated that Franklin may not have been as heavily subscribed to the abolition of slavery as it seems. He did promote the abolitionist cause, it's true, but only after other Founding Fathers did, and only after it became the more prevalent trend in the colonies after the ratification of the Declaration of Independence. In 2004, Waldstreicher said, "Events after 1776, of course, do matter, as do the final acts of great lives. Franklin lived just long enough for his slaves to run away and die off, and for antislavery to become politically safe in his home state."

Quakers were more numerous in Pennsylvania than in any other state or commonwealth. Because they were committed abolitionists, it was politically expedient for Franklin to come out as a leader who likewise opposed slavery.

In addition, the other Founding Fathers, like Washington and even Thomas Jefferson, were softening their support of slavery. When focusing upon the factual lives of these men and their views about slavery, one cannot help but note a contradiction between their words and their acts.

The Gulf Stream Project

Franklin was a communicator and would engage nearly anyone in a conversation. In 1768, when he had been postmaster, he once asked a captain why packets mailed from Great Britain seemed to take longer to arrive than those shipped via other merchant ships. The captain told him that the maps of the Gulf Stream, a massive ocean current in the Atlantic Ocean, had been printed in America, and the British tended to ignore them because of their prejudice against the colonies. Therefore, the British often sailed straight across the Gulf Stream, rather than taking advantage of the west to east current it generates. During the American Revolution, Franklin had maps printed, and distributed them to France, the American ally, for navigational purposes.

In 1786, Franklin consulted with navigators and revised the original maps of the Gulf Stream. Today's experts have examined the revised map that Franklin developed and discovered that it is remarkably accurate.

Unpublicized Inventions

Franklin created a number of devices which he used for his businesses and at home. In 1787, George Washington wrote about a visit he made to Franklin's residence and noticed a machine that Franklin had constructed for ironing flat cloth, rather than using irons. It consisted of a large heated metal plate that was lowered upon another, used for pressing tablecloths and other flat fabrics used for dinner napkins and handkerchiefs.

Another invention occurred when Benjamin Franklin's brother, John, who was sixteen years older than he, developed bladder stones and had to insert a catheter daily to urinate. In those days, they used a rigid metal tube. John found the insertion to be painful and mentioned it to Benjamin. After researching it, Franklin went to a local silversmith and designed a tube made of tiny segments. Historians have credited him with having developed a flexible catheter that would be less painful to insert. However, Franklin was a humble man and indicated that it was invented in 1720, possibly by Francesco Roncelli-Pardino. John indicated that the device was far less painful, and Franklin was pleased.

Another invention was created when Franklin realized the disadvantage of his height. Franklin was less than six feet tall and often had difficulty reaching books on higher shelves. So, he altered a chair using a reversible seat, converting it into a small stepladder. In addition, he also designed an extension arm with two prongs on the end. The prongs could be opened and closed by pulling on a cord. This gadget is similar to the grabbers used today. Franklin used to take one or another of those inventions with him when he went to his library in Philadelphia. No doubt it must have been amusing to the other library patrons to see this older gentleman carrying one of these items on his visits there.

When he went to the downtown library at night, Franklin noticed that the street lights were much dimmer on his way home. These lamps had to be lit each night by the lamplighter, who also needed to clean them. The lights consisted of glass globes equipped with a wick that was fed by a container of whale oil. As the hours passed, the globe would become darker, as it filled with the carbon residue from the burning. In order to resolve the problem, Franklin ventilated the lamp by placing a long glass funnel in it that could channel the smoke upwards. Then he inserted crevices into the bottom to provide a more efficient air flow. They used some in Philadelphia, and those lights stayed bright until morning. In addition, Franklin also praised the use of permanent lights at the base of outside steps.

After pondering the subject of night lighting, it occurred to him that there would be less need for that during the summer when dawn came earlier. In an essay called "An Economic Project," Franklin suggested setting the clocks one hour back to take advantage of the extra daylight. Today, many countries use Daylight Savings Time for that very purpose.

He also theorized the design of a clock that is simpler. The clockworks on this "Benjamin Franklin Clock" ran on the rotation of three interior wheels with teeth. It quite accurately measured the quarter-hour, the half-hour, and full hour. It measured the minutes as well. Although Franklin never actually wrote about it, he discussed it with a Dutch physiologist, Jan Ingenhousz, and another friend from England, James Ferguson. Ferguson designed the clock according to Franklin's discussion and later improved it, much to Franklin's delight.

While living in London, Franklin was astounded by the number of misspellings that occurred in written material. So, he felt that a spelling reform was needed. Seeing that certain letters can sound differently, he created a phonetic alphabet. It had lowercase letters, but he eliminated the consonants c, j, q, x, w, and y. His difficulty with those letters was the fact that there were various ways of pronouncing them and were redundant. For example, hard "c" could sound like a "k," and the soft "c" sounded like an "s." To those, he added six letters and even had typesets manufactured showing what they looked like.

For the vowels, he used a double vowel to signify long vowels. For example, "remeen" meant "remain." Linguists have examined Franklin's proposals but found some inconsistencies in it. In 1789, Franklin wrote to Noah Webster regarding it. Webster was already in the process of updating the English language and spoke to Franklin who was attending some of his lectures. The greatest stumbling block to the promulgation of Franklin's new alphabet was the unavailability of the types needed to print the written pieces. In time, Franklin lost interest in the project because of its inconvenience.

The Death of Benjamin Franklin

In his declining years, Benjamin Franklin was somewhat hunched over and dressed very plainly. He was mostly bald and wore no hat. Walking or standing for any period of time was painful for him. Franklin had the property around his house redesigned with a number of winding gravel walkways interspersed with flowering bushes and trees. Under the shade, there were tea tables at which he entertained friends. Many of his friends were those he knew from the Philadelphia or Constitutional Convention. Franklin and they played cards, chess, and cribbage. Sarah Franklin Bache, his only daughter, lived there with him along with three of her children, and they enjoyed plenty of family time together.

Besides spending time with friends and family, Franklin also enjoyed bathing and felt it was healthy for him. It was because it relieves the symptoms of gout which he had for many years. Although he was corpulent, he also admitted that he was indolent. Toward his later years, he made it a point to walk around his rooms for nearly an hour if possible. Unfortunately, the pain and swelling from his gout often made him stop, and those episodes could last up to a full week, making Franklin occasionally bedridden.

Gout is caused by an excessive accumulation of uric acid that isn't efficiently excreted. It can be caused by eating too much red meat, seafood, or organ meat. Obesity intensifies it. As he aged, he developed boils. Most likely, they came about due to a build-up of uric acid from gout, although he attributed it to "dropsy." Nevertheless, he continued to read avidly and frequently wrote letters to the authors, who were pleased to hear from this well-known man. When he was on his deathbed in 1790, George Washington sent him a letter. In it, he said, in part:

> You have the pleasing consolation to know that you have not lived in vain...Be assured that, so long as I retain my memory, you will be thought of with respect, veneration and affection by your sincere friend, George Washington.

When Franklin became more debilitated from his illness and infirmity, he started developing sore throats, had trouble talking, and could only eat barley. While he attended the conventions, he fell several times trying to keep up with the younger men. However, his call to duty was something he felt compelled to do for his country.

About three weeks before his death, Dr. John Jones presented a report on the failing health of Benjamin Franklin in the *Pennsylvania Gazette*. In his report, he said that Franklin had an extremely high fever, a persistent pain in his chest, a chronic cough, and had difficulty breathing.

Like his brother John, Franklin developed stones in his bladder. Surgeons of the 18th century were able to perform procedures to remedy that, but Franklin felt that he was too old and it wasn't worth the cost of having the surgery performed. He had frequent colds and fits of vomiting. An abscess developed in one of his lungs and burst, causing excruciating pain. Afterward, his pain thankfully left him. He was exhausted and became extremely lethargic. The clinicians today indicate that he most likely suffered from pleurisy and empyema, which is caused by an increase of pus in the lungs and also caused by a bacterial infection, probably due to the burst abscess. His last words were, "A dying man can do nothing easily."

On April 17, 1790, he died quietly.

The *Pennsylvania Gazette* and many other national and overseas publications carried his obituary:

> Died on Saturday night in the 85th year of his age, the illustrious BENJAMIN FRANKLIN. The world has been so long in possession of such extraordinary proofs of the singular abilities and virtues of this FRIEND OF MANKIND that it is impossible for a newspaper to increase his fame, or to convey his name to a part of the civilized globe where it is not already known and admired.

In 1728, Franklin actually wrote his own epitaph which read:

> The body of B. Franklin, Printer, like the cover of an old book, its contents torn out, and script of its lettering and gilding lies here, food for worms. But the work shall not be wholly lost; for it will, as he believ'd, appear once more in a new and more prefect edition, corrected and amended by the author.

The House of Representatives adopted the suggestions of young James Madison to wear symbols of mourning for one month. However, the Senate did not, due to the influence of John Adams and Arthur Lee, who still harbored antipathy toward him. Both Adams and Lee had often spread negative sentiments about him particularly after they were in France with him to negotiate the formulation of the Treaty of Paris. They had been disedified by his lack of eloquence in dress later in life and his casual manners, as well as being morally offended by his comradery with women. They were likewise offended by the political stance of his grandson, Benjamin Franklin Bache, who was a staunch anti-Federalist.

Upon hearing about Franklin's death, the French National Assembly announced a month of mourning in honor of Benjamin Franklin, calling him "the genius who freed America and shed torrents of light on Europe." Count Mirabeau, a French member of the Assemblies in France and supporter of the French Revolution, knew of Franklin through the Marquis de Lafayette. About Franklin, Mirabeau said, "He was able to restrain thunderbolts and tyrants."

After Franklin's death, there was a massive crowd of 20,000 who came to the funeral. That was an astounding number of people in those early days.

Legacy

Benjamin Franklin lived his life openly. He was vulnerable, but his vulnerability was his strength. He had the courage of a warrior who needed no shield. In his autobiography, he listed the principles by which he always wanted to live. These he called the Thirteen Necessary Virtues:

> 1. TEMPERANCE. Drink not to indulgence; drink not to elevation.

> There were never any reports of Ben Franklin being drunk, but he did enjoy wine. In 1779, he said, "Behold the rain which descends from heaven and is incorporated into grapes to be changed into wine; a constant proof the God loves us and loves to see us happy."

> 2. SILENCE. Speak not but what may benefit others or yourself; avoid trifling conversation

> When Franklin was pondering political and scientific issues, he was absolutely silent, but shared his views freely with those whom he knew would be affected by following the suggestions that he thought might be beneficial to others. Despite the fact that he wrote and designed numerous inventions, Franklin never took out any patents on them. He said, "…as we enjoy great advantages from the inventions of others, we should be glad of an opportunity to serve others by

any invention of ours; and this we should do freely and generously."

3. ORDER. Let all things have their places; let each part of your business have its time.

Franklin kept meticulous records of everything he did. He could produce documentation for all the logistical proposals that he made and accompanied his actions with a written record of it.

4. RESOLUTION. Resolve to perform what you ought; perform without fail what you resolve.

Franklin's entire life was directed toward a goal. When he was sent as a troubleshooter and an ambassador to England and France, he worked feverishly toward accomplishing his goals. When he had to appear before the Privy Council in England, he was nearly 70 years old, but stood up the entire time and persevered throughout the lengthy procedure like a 20-year-old, because that was his job.

5. FRUGALITY. Make no expense but to do good to others or yourself; waste nothing.

During the boycott of British goods prior to the American Revolution, Franklin instructed all Americans to manufacture their own goods. He also canceled his own personal orders for English goods and instructed his own staff to manage with what they had on hand or create a substitute.

6. INDUSTRY. Lose no time; be always employed in something useful; but off all unnecessary actions.

Benjamin Franklin lived until he was 84. During his lifetime, he did thousands of useful things to the point that records of his work fill volumes. He never stopped. For example, when he went to the Tun Tavern in Philadelphia, he made it a point to combine business with pleasure. He used the tavern as a place where he could hold meetings and recruit troops, as well as enjoy the company of others.

7. SINCERITY. Use no hurtful deceit; think innocently and justly, and, if you speak, speak accordingly.

In the annals of history, there is no record of Franklin ever making false claims about another person. In fact, he was so straightforward that some of his detractors were taken back by his "plain speech."

8. JUSTICE. Wrong none by doing injuries, or omitting the benefits that are your duty.

When he objected to someone's view, Franklin always gave the other the benefit of the doubt.

9. MODERATION. Avoid extremes; forbear resenting injuries so much as you think they deserve.

Franklin was never considered to be a hostile man. In responding to a politician who disagreed with him, he always addressed the issue without resorting to personal insult.

10. CLEANLINESS. Tolerate no uncleanliness in body, clothes or habitation.

Although there's no record of his habits related to cleanliness, no comment was ever made about him to the effect that he was sloppy. However, when he crossed New Jersey to get to Philadelphia, the rain was so constant that, no doubt, he arrived disheveled and soaked!

11. TRANQUILITY. Be not disturbed at trifles, or at accidents common or unavoidable.

During his experiments, Franklin made many errors, like shocking himself when he flew his famous kite with the key. That never stopped him. It was his sense of tranquility that gave him persistence.

12. CHASTITY. Rarely use venery but for health or offspring, never to dullness, weakness, or injury of your own or another's reputation.

Franklin was a "ladies' man," and rumors abounded about his promiscuity, although not all of his relationships were sexual, and perhaps none were.

13. HUMILITY. Imitate Jesus and Socrates.

It is difficult to compare Franklin to Jesus, but he was just as deep a thinker as Socrates and tried to imitate the qualities of Jesus.

His Will

Benjamin Franklin owned a great deal of land which he divided up and bequeathed to his family. In addition, he divided up his buildings and wealth at the time of his death among his survivors with the exception of his eldest son William, with whom he had a serious falling out late in life. William already owned some land in Pennsylvania, which—of course—was rightfully his. He restricted his will to the forgiveness of any outstanding debts William owed and gave him the papers and books William already had possession of.

Franklin was particularly fond of a portrait given to him by King Louis XVI of France, containing 100 precious diamonds. That he gave to his daughter, Sarah Franklin Bache. In his will, it was clear he tried not to forget anyone. That even included some of the people who worked for him in the printing and publishing business.

To his grandchild, Benjamin Franklin Bache, he bequeathed his printing press and equipment. His grandson had pursued printing as a career and was already publishing a newspaper, the *Philadelphia Aurora*. He was a writer, too, who wrote about politics like his grandfather and even tried his hand at poetry.

Benjamin Franklin bequeathed to Boston and Philadelphia 1,000 pounds to be placed in a 200-year trust fund. More than $2,000,000 had been collected in the Philadelphia trust by 1990. It loaned money to the people of Philadelphia and was used to finance their mortgage loans as well. The Boston trust fund had accumulated about $5,000,000, which was used to finance the Franklin Institute of Boston, and what remained was used to maintain the institution.

The most precious item that he gave was invisible to the eye but known to every living American. It was his ceaseless effort to assure that America will remain free.

Conclusion

Benjamin Franklin was, by far, one of the most versatile polymaths the world has ever known. He wasn't a "generalist" or a "jack of all trades," in the sense that he knew a little bit about everything. He knew a *great deal* about a wide variety of fields—science, philosophy, medicine, politics, finances, human relations, chemistry, religion, physical science, publishing, humor, writing, printing, and even candle making! Franklin was the Leonardo da Vinci of his day, although he never considered himself to be a genius (though he probably was). Franklin simply exploded with boundless curiosity.

He lived during one of the most tumultuous periods of America. Not only was he instrumental in bringing about freedom and liberty for the United States, but he assisted in the birth of a new nation. When there were difficulties, he didn't fret; he dealt with them. This was a surprising characteristic, given the fact that he demonstrated all the traits of an average—but rather wild—adolescent. His incessant addiction to knowledge motivated him to become self-taught in many subjects.

Unlike other thinkers, he believed in testing out his beliefs and theories in a practical setting. At a time when there was no such thing as mass communication, his viewpoints spread across Europe at a breathtaking pace. In his roles as ambassador, emissary, and agent, he spent over twenty years abroad, but frequently arrived overseas only to find out that the people in Europe were already knowledgeable about his accomplishments. While in England and France, he promoted and publicized the values of the American Enlightenment way of thinking.

Benjamin Franklin was one of the most versatile and productive Americans of the 18th century. As a Founding Father of the United States and political theorist, he helped formulate a framework for a democratic republic and guided a new nation toward becoming a bulwark of freedom. In addition, he stimulated scientific curiosity to the point that it fostered the proliferation of invention and innovation. Franklin is still important today because he showed generations to come that curiosity and freedom of thought has everlasting rewards.

Read more biographies from Captivating History

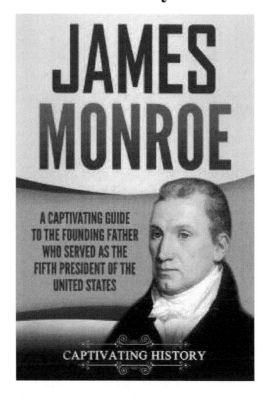

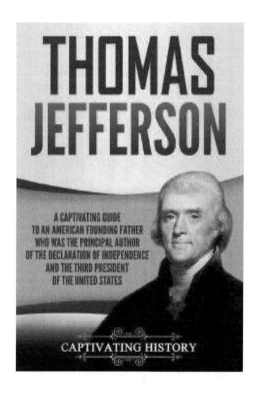

A CAPTIVATING
GUIDE TO ONE OF THE
FOUNDING FATHERS
OF THE UNITED
STATES OF AMERICA

ALEXANDER
HAMILTON

CAPTIVATING HISTORY

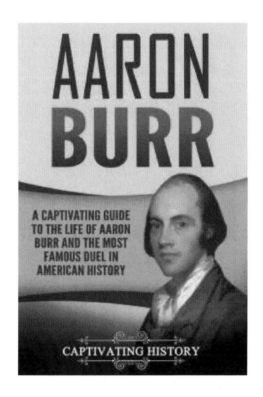

AARON BURR

A CAPTIVATING GUIDE TO THE LIFE OF AARON BURR AND THE MOST FAMOUS DUEL IN AMERICAN HISTORY

CAPTIVATING HISTORY

References

Adams, J., Taylor, R. (ed) "Papers of John Adams, Vol 2" Retrieved from http://oll.libertyfund.org/titles/adams-the-works-of-john-adams-vol-5-defence-of-the-constitutions-vols-ii-and-iii

"Benjamin Franklin: Enlightenment Archetype" Retrieved from https://atlassociety.org/commentary/commentary-blog/4934-benjamin-franklin-enlightenment-archetype

"Ben Franklin: His Autobiography 1706-1757" Retrieved from http://www.let.rug.nl/usa/biographies/benjamin-franklin/

"Benjamin Franklin's Mission to London, 1757-1762," *Journal of the American Revolution.* Retrieved from https://allthingsliberty.com/2017/09/benjamin-franklins-mission-london-1757-1762/

"Colonists Respond to the Quartering Act of 1765," Making the Revolution: America 176-1791" Retrieved from http://americainclass.org/sources/makingrevolution/crisis/text4/quart eringactresponse1766.pdf

Fleming, T. J. "A Touch of France/Taking Paris by Storm: Benjamin Franklin, Founding Father and First Ambassador to France,"

Retrieved from https://www.medicographia.com/2014/06/a-touch-of-france-taking-paris-by-storm-benjamin-franklin-american-founding-father-and-first-ambassador-to-france/

"Flashback: Lamps and Illuminants," *Collectors' Weekly.* Retrieved from https://www.collectorsweekly.com/articles/lamps-and-illuminants/

Ford, P. L. (1921) *The Many-Sided Franklin.* Century Company

Franklin, B. "Benjamin Franklin and the Stamp Act Crisis" Retrieved from http://www.digitalhistory.uh.edu/disp_textbook.cfm?smtID=3&psid=152

Franklin, R., Trent, W. P. (ed) (1906) *Benjamin Franklin: His Life* Ginn & Co.

Franklin, B., Bigelow, J. (ed) (1904) *Benjamin Franklin: Digital Version of the Autobiography, Vol. 5* G. P. Putnam

Franklin, B., Sparks, J. (ed.) (1882) *The Works of Benjamin Franklin: Containing Several Political and Historical Tracts Not Included in Any Former Edition and Many Letters, Official and Private, Vol. 4* Benjamin Franklin Stevens

"Franklin's Papers," *Packard Humanities Institute* Retrieved from http://franklinpapers.org/framedVolumes.jsp

"From Benjamin Franklin to Richard Jackson, 25 June 1764 Retrieved from https://founders.archives.gov/documents/Franklin/01-11-02-0064#BNFN-01-11-02-0064-fn-0002

"George Grenville" Retrieved from http://www.ouramericanrevolution.org/index.cfm/people/view/pp0012

Huth, E. J. (2006) Benjamin Franklin's Place in the History of Medicine," *The James Lind Library.* Retrieved from http://www.jameslindlibrary.org/articles/benjamin-franklins-1706-1790-place-in-the-history-of-medicine/

Kidd, T. S. (June 28, 201) "How Benjamin Franklin, a deist, and Became a Founding Father of a Unique Kind of American Faith," *The Washington Post*

Lapsansky-Werner, E., Talbott, T. (ed.) (2005) "At the End, an Abolitionist?" From *Benjamin Franklin in Search of a Better World*, pps. 273-296 Yale University Press

McClay, G. "A Long Road to Abolitionism: Benjamin Franklin's Transformation on Slavery," California State University (unpub. ms.) Retrieved from https://csueastbay-dspace.calstate.edu/bitstream/handle/10211.3/196230/Gregory.McClayThesis.pdf?sequence=1

Morgan, E. S. (2003) *Benjamin Franklin* Yale University Press

"Last Will and Testament of Benjamin Franklin" Retrieved from https://www.constitution.org/primarysources/lastwill.html

Ruppert, B. "Ben Franklin's Mission to London, 1757-1762" Retrieved from https://allthingsliberty.com/2017/09/benjamin-franklins-mission-london-1757-1762/

Scharf, J. T. (1884) *History of Philadelphia, 1609-1884, Vol. 3* L. H. Everts & Co.

Schultze, C. "Why Was Benjamin Franklin's Basement Filled with Skeletons?" *Smithsonian Magazine* Retrieved from https://www.smithsonianmag.com/smart-news/why-was-benjamin-franklins-basement-filled-with-skeletons-524521/

Waldstreicher, D. (2005) *Runaway America* Ferrar, Straus and Giroux

Weems, M. L. (1873) *The Life of Benjamin Franklin: With Many Choice Anecdotes and Admirable Sayings of this Great Man* Uriah Hunts & Sons

Whipple, W. (1916) *The Young Benjamin* Franklin Henry Altemus Co.

"William Pitt's Defense of the American Colonies," *Colonial Williamsburg.* Retrieved from http://www.history.org/almanack/life/politics/pitt.cfm

Wood, G.S. (2005) *The Americanization of Benjamin Franklin* Penguin

Made in the USA
Middletown, DE
05 December 2021